MATERIAL INNOVATION
ARCHITECTURE

With 415 colour illustrations

CONTENTS

Preface by
George M. Beylerian   6

VISUAL NARRATIVE **Hariri Pontarini Architects** 8

Introduction by
Gail Peter Borden, AIA, Borden Partnership 10

For each project a list of related materials has been included. The numbers are Material ConneXion's MC Index numbers which are a six-digit reference that is unique to each material in the library. The first four digits correspond to a specific manufacturer, in chronological order of acceptance into the archive. The last two digits are the chronological reference of each specific material from that manufacturer. The MC numbers are the basis for how searches are conducted through the thousands of materials that exist in the library. For more information visit www.materialconnexion.com/books.

First published in the United Kingdom
in 2014 by Thames & Hudson Ltd,
181A High Holborn, London WC1V 7QX

Material Innovation: Architecture © 2014
Material ConneXion Inc.

MCX
Material ConneXion®

A SANDOW Company

British Library Cataloguing-in-Publication Data
A catalogue record for this book is available from the British Library

ISBN 978-0-500-29128-3

Printed in China by Shanghai Offset Printing Products Limited

To find out about all our publications, please visit
www.thamesandhudson.com.
There you can subscribe to our e-newsletter, browse or download our current catalogue, and buy any titles that are in print.

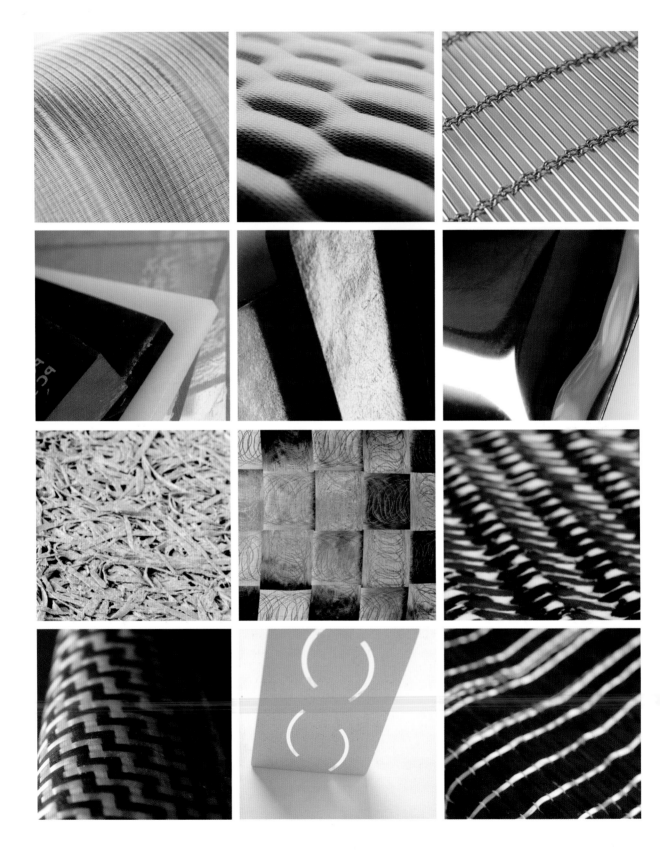

PREFACE

BY GEORGE M. BEYLERIAN

When I founded Material ConneXion in 1997, the idea of a library of advanced, innovative materials where architects and designers could come in search of not merely materials but inspiration and innovation was unheard of. These days, access to and knowledge about materials is almost commonplace. But, back then, building a forum for exchange between creatives, engineers, and material manufacturers was something of a radical act.

No longer. Today, Material ConneXion offers a global resource for material research whose influence and expertise informs a wide range of corporate, cultural, and consumer sectors, and touches literally hundreds of thousands of people daily. Beyond the experience of visiting the library—now located in ten cities around the globe—publications, both print and digital, offer a meaningful way to share the library's vast material intelligence with professionals, educators, and students.

This first book in a ten-part series published by Thames & Hudson, which specializes in exceptional illustrated books, is, then, the synthesis of decades' worth of Material ConneXion knowledge that points the way toward the most original and daring visions driving architecture today. When we think about the future of materials, it is obvious to me that those who have recently contributed in so many remarkable ways to our physical landscape should be celebrated for their contributions to the here, now, and tomorrow.

What sets this book, and all subsequent volumes in the series, apart is its focus on specific categories of materials that reflect the most rigorous, intellectually inquisitive questions being posed today by a given discipline. Whether it is architecture, fashion, or transportation, innovation is the driver that inspires creatives, scientists, engineers, and manufacturers to imagine and pursue the optimal material for each specific application so as to elevate the objects, spaces, and experiences with which we live and work.

This is an exciting time for design education to be forward-thinking and to capitalize on the unprecedented potential afforded by libraries such as that of Material ConneXion, especially as technology gives students greater opportunities for collective experimentation. Emerging practitioners are empowered not only by software but also by the knowledge made possible by such books as this, that are essential for learning by doing. Again and again, the same thrill I felt when I first started exploring materials, the sense of expectancy about what new ideas might be sparked, is as potent as ever. Every new introduction to the library recalibrates our imagination and sets the stage for that great collaboration when art and science come together to seize the moment and create something new.

INTRODUCTION

BY GAIL PETER BORDEN, AIA
BORDEN PARTNERSHIP

Materiality has re-established its essential role as the premise for the making of architecture. By confronting the question of what are shared current architectural interests among various practices and contemporary methods of teaching, a material discourse has emerged that fundamentally revolves around physical matter, material, and the process-based design decisions that emerge through making.

The essence of architectural making is found in material systems. "What" we make, and "how" we make, are essential to the definition and production of form, function, and perception. Materials are the essence of what architecture actually is.

The historical relationship between the material and the act of making was one of locality. Construction was rooted in tradition and provided both formal and technical solutions for how to build and what to build out of. The Industrial Revolution modified this localized relationship with the mass production of construction materials and the shifting of typologies, complexities and scales with which architecture needed to respond. Emerging networks of mass transportation and technological advancements, combined with large urban working populations, collectively permitted new scales of production able to provide an even blanket of availability, resulting in a seemingly appropriate universal applicability of new materials, tectonics, and associated forms. The architect was now

suddenly presented with a palette of materials allowing for selection based on diverse considerations such as cost, structural performance, durability, form, and effect. This began a detachment from material sources and a transition to application based upon intellectual desires. The composition of architecture became bound by the selection, application and detailing of materials, with locality no longer being the deciding factor.

Emerging fabrication and construction technologies along with innovation in material science have further expanded architectural flexibility and individuation. Innate physical properties can now be overcome. Balanced by technological innovation, the expansion of potential application is ever increasing, fragmenting what had seemed to be stable traditions of use and application. Nostalgic perceptions of limits and abilities have been cast aside as the design application limits of a particular material are no longer seen as inherent within the material itself, but rather as functions of surrounding processes. Tools and materials have become inseparable and indistinct from one another. There is no material that is unmediated.

The new relationship established through the re-conceptualization of material roles has established a generation of architects operating along similar lines, grounded in an intense desire to make real things. Varied in technique and scale, method and intent, yet having a collective connection to the physical translation of idea into matter, they are a generation fascinated with thinking through making. Challenging both technology and physicality to further the relationship of material to architecture, their convictions root the need for the actual physicality to engage the interrelations of material with space and experience. Their design method does not necessarily require a constructed result, but the physicality of the real is ingrained in their thinking and process. The method of working is ultra-real, demanding a physical response and challenging the thinking out of the abstract and into the bluntly real.

The foresight of this generation of emerging practitioners stems from their innately digitally savvy design methods, which allow for a seamlessly integrated engagement and permit their work to move beyond the formalist trapping of method and technique. The result is the derivation of new boundaries; techniques that engage craft and technology to hybridize architecture and making. This direct relationship allows for an interest in the material proper, the process of its manipulation and the assembly technique, all as issues to produce form and effect. As a result, the physical nature of materials and their interrelationship with tools has facilitated a new chapter in architectural thinking and practice. In an era of explosive technological advancements in both what we make things out of (matter) and also how we make, materials have led to a new discourse about process and product.

What something is to be made of is foundational to design thinking. The origins establish the result. Experimentation with tactile and physical properties has allowed the designer to reassert a connection to making long since divorced from the purview of architects. The confrontation of the "real," of the physical, the associative and the intrinsic limitations and physical qualities of matter, positions the designer back in a direct dialogue with matter. In this conversation, architects now challenge expectations and battle with practical physicality. Matter as a form of resistance establishes an aggressive interface: cutting, shearing, bending, rolling, extruding, milling, punching, crimping, drilling . . . all allow for and establish the parameters of engagement. Tools become the mediator. Their collaboration establishes process through the interface of tool and material, allowing for the production, transposition and realization of new forms. These allow for reconsideration of performative qualities from the material to the assembly, and relate to the newness of perceptory and technical results alike. As a result evolutions have happened at four key scales.

MATERIAL PRODUCT

In the late twentieth century, the notion of material was aligned with a humanist tradition associated with the craftsperson. It was neither considered "avant-garde" nor recognized as a part of a conceptual project. Instead it was relegated to a technical discourse. This position is no longer tenable. The connection between the idea and the material is essential. Craft is not a base consideration, but the connection between the mind and the body through material.

The last decade has witnessed a shift toward a more practical model of architecture. The discipline of architecture has engaged a new literalism of architectural technique and production that focuses on material performance, to work through the real instead of ignoring it. As the architectural discipline begins what we can again term a more direct relationship with materiality, our disciplinary

Pages 10 and 13 "Light Frames"
by Gail Peter Borden.

Below and page 17 "Density
Frames" by Gail Peter Borden.

"Light Frames" and "Density Frames"
are iterative installations investigating
lightness. As recombinations of the same
material and system, they are pop-up
site-based inquiries into material, light,
and space through experience.

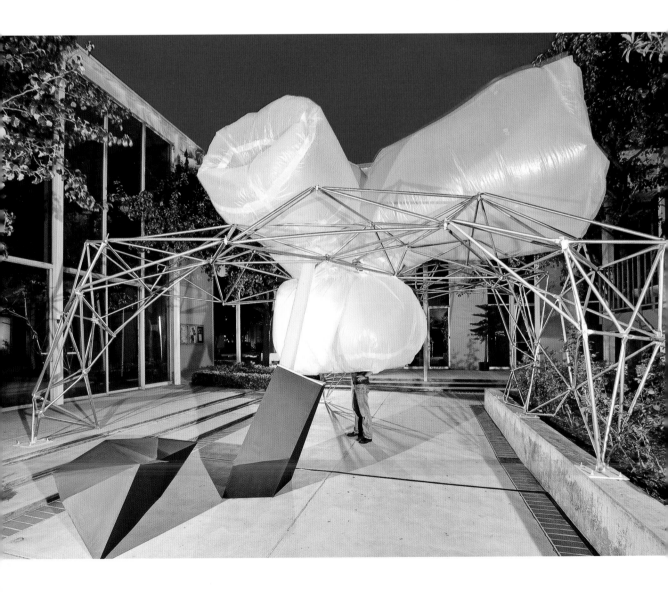

challenge is now to grapple with our re-emerging interest in physical form as a derivative of how it is made, and of what, as a way of playing with a post-postmodern need for realism and a post-digital stance no longer infatuated with computation as a destination in its own right but now focusing on a need for quantifiable techniques and evaluation through material. These emerging and required reorganizations of architectural thinking and action through matter reveal both our current opportunities and our mounting responsibility with greater clarity. In responding to these issues, we can propose the possibility of a conceptual architecture of substance, of matter, by manipulating and deploying an array of innovative techniques and methods each with unavoidable material circumstances.

Material matter has itself evolved. Through the advanced innovation of chemical understanding, manufacturing processes and assembly techniques have revolutionized "products" to hyper-advanced levels of customization and complexity. The matter that we start with now has a sophistication that can no longer be fully understood by a single designer or craftsman across all material types and requires a new sophisticated synthesis of specific craftsman with manufacturer with designer.

PRACTICE AS RESEARCH

This hybrid model has led to a flourishing of experimental practices that root themselves in the fertile territory of material inquiry. Focused on the installation, their work rides the breaking edge of practice, pushing the boundary of application and experimentation with innovative and aggressive schemes. Limited in scope of responsibility, these projects emerge as true design research, challenging how we make things, what they are made of, what we can expect from objects we make, and how they can inform the complexity and ever-increasing responsibility and opportunity of contemporary practice.

TOOLS AND PROCESS

To parallel the expansion of simple products, the expansion of systems of manipulation through tools of operation has exploded the capability and the precision of how we make. Advanced computational techniques, from parametric modeling to direct design-based processing, have changed the scale of how we manage the complexity of information and form. The ability to integrate sophisticated feedback loops in the process of design extends the calibration of formal and physical response to embed intelligence into the process. The new sophistications of digital fabrication have expanded the opportunity for individuation and mass customization.

Fundamentally, the machine simply makes, performing a task for a certain amount of time. The machine now endowed with expanded capabilities can perform multiple actions. It does not care if it is making one thousand copies of a single part or a thousand individually unique parts. It can customize, iterate, and allow variation with ease. The result is formwork, components, elements of all scales and materials that can be fundamentally changed at the scale of the unit. The object as a manufactured product is no longer preordained. It now becomes a collaborative dialogue between the innate physical characteristics of material matter (the ability to burn, bend, support, be transparent, repel moisture, provide thermal or acoustical insulation, and so on) and the capacity of the tool (how deep it can cut, the scale of the operation, the profile of a bit, the duration of a cut, and so on).

These guidelines now establish a broader terrain of thinking where the result is determined in scope of understanding and innovation of system manipulation. These two together become the new parameter. The designer need understand not simple products but rather system rules. The rules then become the moment of insertion where the vision and artful intent of architecture move beyond the simple pragmatics of function, reaching and extending for the emotive intention of design and allowing for the sublime.

ASSEMBLY

The fourth area of innovation comes then in the understanding of assembly. When transitions from element to element and position to position are no longer ignored as givens but instead are problematized as creative potential, part-to-whole systems of composition are scrutinized. In other words, the singular scale of an image is exposed as incomplete: part, whole, surface, and unit become equally available for consideration at multiple scales, and Beaux-Arts overarching compositional models are undermined in favor of scalar and discrete situational relationships. Rooted in geometry, the systems of aggregation and assembly are essential to the scale of building. As constructs larger than the human scale, they require production off site, movement to the site, and then assembly. The required aggregation that emerges privileges the role of tectonics in any architectural composition: regardless of the connection's celebration or denial, the interrelationships of part to part, a material assembly is essential. In most systems, the interrelationship establishes a new system. Bricks and mortar combine to create fields; courses and binding patterns systematize to become more legible and familiar than their components.

Inserting innovation and intelligence into this phase of the design process allows an intense opportunity to reconsider traditional norms. From the varied rotation of a masonry unit to dynamic skins of variably perforated metal, new material effects emerge from the pattern, system, and geometric combination of piece to piece.

The time for material consideration has never been more fertile. Every architect must deal with the innate issue of what something is made of. Even in drawing and representation, abstract, two-dimensional, and monochromatic, we intrinsically establish scale and thickness which imply a quality and associative materiality.

This book serves as an introductory catalog of contemporary tactics. One of a series focused on diverse disciplines, it highlights themes and subsets of approaches undertaken by some of the most innovative and avant-garde practices operating in the global landscape. Though each case study is set within a different context (both physical and cultural), responding to varied programs and budgets, they collectively privilege material process in their thinking and making. Rooted in the same dialogue of material to tool to assembly, their innovations provide engaging case studies of specific and elegant solutions, but more importantly, suggest a methodology, ripe with opportunity, essential in premise, and on the frontier of contemporary practice. Material making is the new architecture.

STEVEN HOLL ARCHITECTS

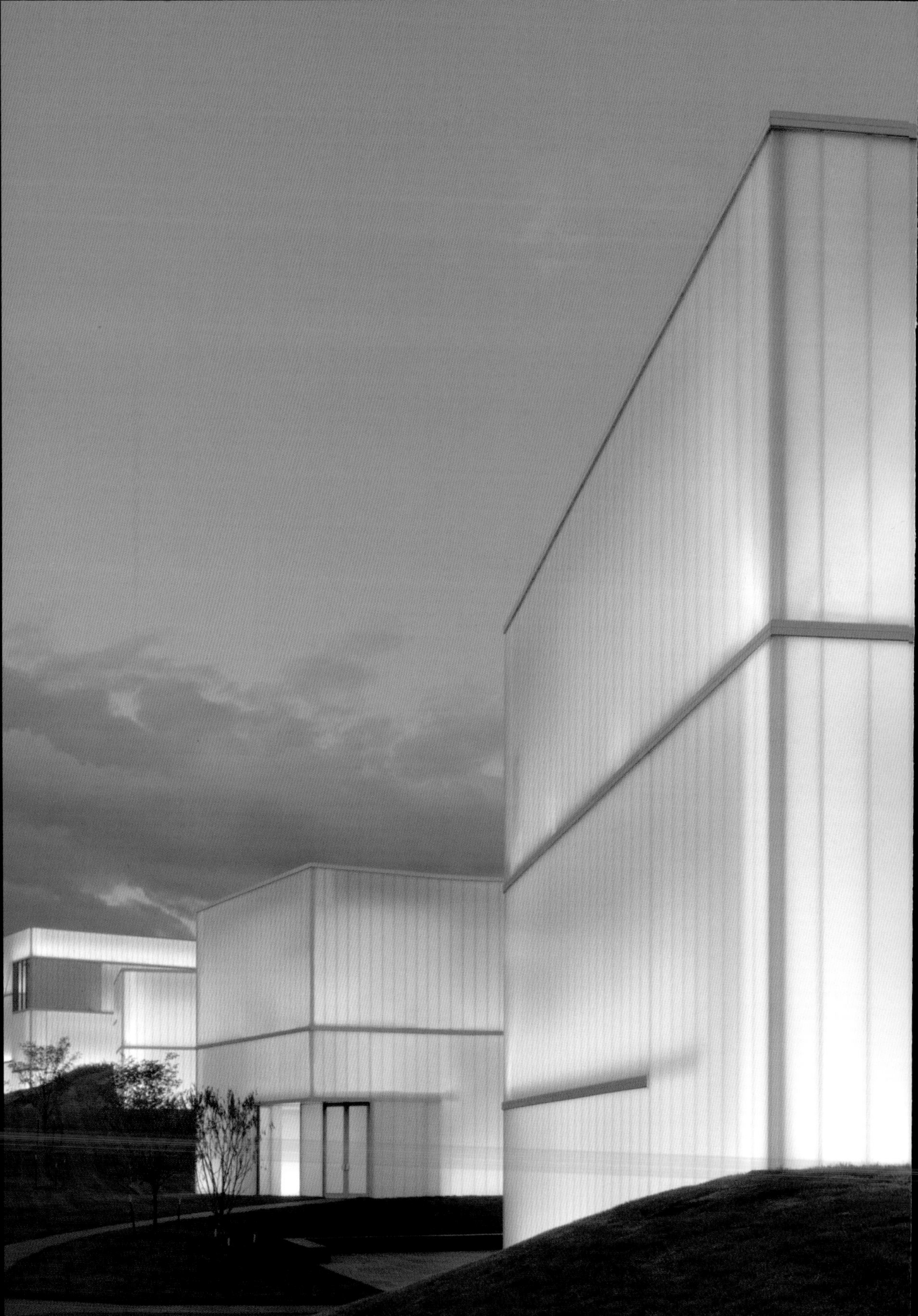

CHAPTER 1
GLASS & CERAMICS

To follow the trajectory of glass and its use in many areas of our lives is to see a material that is both celebrated for and limited by its fundamental properties. Transparency and durability give it universal appeal in glazing, yet its fragility and weight force this transparency into limited applications, with extensive structural support and hardware still essential for its safe and effective use. We are also at a crossroads for the material—a lack of transformative innovation in some of its main limitations has led to polymers overtaking it in many important categories, with architectural glazing being one of the few areas where it still commands an almost exclusive monopoly.

There are some promising trends for this group of materials, however, which have grown out of the consumer electronics industry. The use of super-thin, tough, and scratch-resistant screens has renewed interest in glass being used for our displays. Coupled with an increasing desire that more surfaces (glazing, countertops, desks, appliance control panels, shop fronts, and so on) should exhibit the smart aspect of touch screens, this means that a new generation of glass-based surfaces is being developed. In parallel, and somewhat synergistically with this trend, has been the innovation of glazing interlayers: the material between glazing panes rather than the glass itself. This means advances in the use of glazing as a system, which offer improved insulation, heat reflection, stiffness, and impact-resistance enhancement to the glass, by added function through sealing layers of durable glass. After a period of relative stagnation in glazing advancement, there is a completely new way of seeing glass.

Advances in glazing and smart surfaces are complemented by age-old techniques such as glass casting, shown here in a panel made of glass rods melted and fused together.

NEW FORMS IN GLAZING

Challenging what the basic glazing panel can withstand, a number of developments show new ideas in this area. The limits of how much glass can be bent while still maintaining good strength can be seen in buildings such as New York's IRC Tower on Manhattan's West Side, where Gehry and Partners used the material's inherent elasticity to form curved structural panels. The roof of the Victoria and Albert Museum in London by MUMA Architects is another example of this technique. The glass is "cold bent," which means that if it were removed from its frame in the structure then it would snap back to a flat geometry. Bending gives the material greater impact strength thanks to its increased tension, but it reduces the pane's compressive strength.

"Slumping" the glass to create a structural element in the face of the pane can also increase performance. Glass in glazing is typically flat, but there have been some innovations recently that use the bending or "slumping" of glass following manufacture to create shapes in the pane to improve stiffness. The simple corrugation of cardboard or the creation of ridges in metals increases stiffness in specific directions, and this effect can also be achieved in large panes of glass. The Museum aan de Stroom in Antwerp, Belgium, by Neutelings Riedijk uses corrugation of glass as an additional structural element to improve compressive vertical strength. The Vakko Fashion and Power Media Center in Istanbul, Turkey, by REX has used the slumping process (where glass is repeatedly heated and cooled until it falls into a mold and assumes the mold's form) to create X shapes in the pane to improve stiffness.

CERAMICS

Ceramic materials have been included in this category thanks to the fact that in material science there is no differentiation between the chemistry of a "glass," and the chemistry of a ceramic: it is merely a change in crystal structure. Both fall under the general category of ceramic. When made suitably pure and with a certain crystal structure, other ceramics can also be optically transparent and have very similar properties to "glass." High-end watch faces, space telescope mirrors, and armor use this combination of clarity, heat resistance, and superior durability, but despite new developments that are potentially reducing the cost of these materials—the raw materials are inexpensive but processing is still the cost-determining factor—they have rarely ever been used in architecture. There has, however, been a relative resurgence in the use of ceramic materials as high-tech "smart" façades, using their thermal mass and cooling properties when wet to regulate sunlight, heat, and cold. High-profile projects such as the ceramic rods used on the façade of the New York Times Building by Renzo Piano are examples of this.

Terracotta is also making a comeback, with the use of this porous material to act as an envelope system. Standard glazed and unglazed terracotta tiles are being employed as cladding on buildings such as the Museum of Arts and Design building at 2 Columbus Circle in New York by Allied Works Architecture, and most recently, in large-scale projects such as the King Abdullah University of Science and Technology (KAUST) in Jeddah, Saudi Arabia. Designed by HOK, this uses 120,000 m² (1,290,000 ft²) of terracotta, applied using a flexible aluminum structural frame first prototyped on Berlin's Potsdamer Platz by Renzo Piano in the 1990s. At KAUST, the shape of the terracotta tile has been improved to give better performance. Cone-like forms molded from clay are combined into a flexible wall structure using composite materials to improve energy efficiency. Condensation at night creates evaporative cooling during the day, with the shape of the form and the thermal mass of the clay giving better thermal control. This offers an innovative use of a traditional material.

DIGITAL DISPLAYS

As previously mentioned, there has been much innovation in glass thanks to the consumer electronics industry. With the digital age have come digital screens, together with the desire that these might also be transparent when not in

Stronger, thinner, and smarter glass-ceramics have enabled Perceptive Pixel Inc. (now part of Microsoft) to design large multi-touch displays that anticipate digital surfaces at an architectural scale.

use. The current possibilities for this are high-transparency plastics and glass. To date, Corning's Gorilla Glass, a toughened silica-based screen, has been the "go-to" material for most touch screens and laptop displays, although there are new alternatives that offer similar performance, such as SCHOTT's Xensation. These are materials that can potentially be used for larger digital surfaces and double up as glazing, offering a scratch- and smudge-resistant surface that can be made much thinner but with the same strength as standard glazing or even toughened glass.

Gorilla Glass is one material in an evolution of toughened transparent surfaces that Corning has developed. It is produced through a unique process that pours molten glass (red hot) into a trough that overflows on both sides; the overflow connects underneath the trough and falls as a consistently thin sheet that cools and can then be cut to size. This allows for the creation of very large panes, which can—with sufficient care—be transported to fabrication sites. The toughness is increased by "chemical strengthening," stuffing larger potassium ions into the surface, replacing the smaller silicon ions and thereby making the structure tougher, so that minor scratches do not weaken the glass and so it can be made thinner without breaking. The first generation was a material called Eagle Glass, an alkaline earth boro-aluminosilicate, which was used as an alternative to LCD glass but contained no toxic added arsenic, antimony, barium, or halides. Gorilla Glass is a tougher version, which maintains the superior clarity and surface quality.

Willow Glass, debuted in 2012, evolved from Gorilla Glass and when made much thinner becomes remarkably more flexible. (When made thin, glass is extremely flexible; thin glass fiber can indeed be knitted, but once the surface is scratched then it tends to break easily. This is remedied in glass fiber by coating with plastic and in the Willow Glass by making the surface sufficiently hard so that it is scratch-proof.) Thinner, lighter, flexible glass with the surface hardness to deal with everyday use will push forward flexible devices, but also potentially enable larger, more versatile digital glazing— the glass can be laminated onto lightweight plastics such as polycarbonate for greater toughness, spanning many meters and curving around forms.

INTERLAYERS

It is the *other* materials forming part of the multilayer lamination that actually create the display imagery of this new digital glazing—for instance, the light-emitting polymer

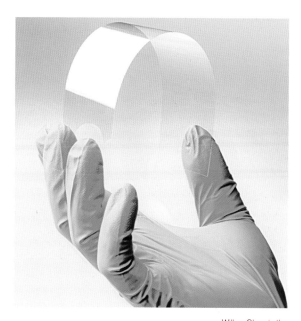

Willow Glass is the third of Corning's products, each thinner and tougher than the last. The surface is extraordinarily scratch-proof and thus it can be made thin enough to bend without breaking.

films, the conductive transparent layers (the current standard in this field for laptops and phones is indium tin oxide, ITO, a thin, clear ceramic, which unfortunately cracks when subjected to flexing—newer flexible versions require a polymer film), and the power sources, all in addition to the surface you actually touch. Current commercially available films that presage the use of this type of smart glass in large-scale applications include electrochromics such as those offered by Sage (recently purchased by global glass powerhouse Saint-Gobain), which can darken to reduce heat gain or to provide privacy, and which have finally become suitably durable and economically manageable so that they are viable for large-scale glazing projects.

SURFACE TREATMENTS

The surface of glass is being treated to reduce the regular need for cleaning. Silver-based antimicrobials and titanium-dioxide-based photocatalytic coatings are deposited onto exterior glazing to create surfaces that are not hospitable to organic matter, keeping them cleaner for longer (although not yet enabling them to forgo cleaning altogether) without sacrificing transparency or durability.

We could well be seeing a renaissance period for glass, a material once thought to be forever constrained by its limitations, now potentially leading the way in an evolution of digital, thin, lightweight surfaces that transcend the idea of glazing altogether.

TOLEDO MUSEUM OF ART GLASS PAVILION

CLIENT
Toledo Museum of Art represented
by the Paratus Group

ARCHITECT
Kazuyo Sejima & Ryue Nishizawa / SANAA

MATERIAL ENGINEER
Front Inc.

LOCATION
Toledo, Ohio, USA

COMPLETION
2006

SIZE
7,000 m² / 75,348 ft² (built area)

MATERIAL
Laminated (PVB) float glass Optiwhite panels
from Pilkington

RELATED MATERIALS
MC# 5554-02, MC# 5613-01, MC# 6851-01

opposite The low-iron glass panes
of the Toledo Glass Pavilion were
sent to Shenzhen in China for
slumping, tempering, laminating,
and fabrication into finished panels.
The undulating profile of the 2-cm
(0.75-in.) thick interior glass
panels gives the space a sense
of labyrinthine lightness, which
dissolves at the edges of the
courtyards where visitors can
look up at the sky.

Composed of virtually colorless, see-through walls, the Glass Pavilion at the Toledo Museum of Art melds beautifully with its setting and purpose, nodding in both materiality and transparency to the midwestern city's history as a major center of glass production. The strikingly simple horizontal structure set within a grove of oak trees is the first building outside of Japan designed by Kazuyo Sejima and Ryue Nishizawa, partners in the Tokyo-based firm SANAA whose designs consistently show a mastery of lightness and clarity due, in large measure, to their innovative use of glass.

Rendered with skillful economy and restraint, the 4.5-meter (15-foot) high rectangular form incorporates galleries featuring the museum's world-renowned glass collection, a multipurpose meeting room, and a glass-blowing hot shop framed by a concrete floor and thin steel roof. Three simple interior courtyards divide these spaces, opening up views of the sky and allowing light to infuse the interiors. A sense of continuous space that blurs the difference between inside and out results from enormous sheets of glass used for both the envelope and interior wall partitions. These expansive single panes, produced in Austria and custom-curved in southern China, eliminate corners and, coupled with minimal bonding via silicone beading, offer the maximum amount of transparency possible.

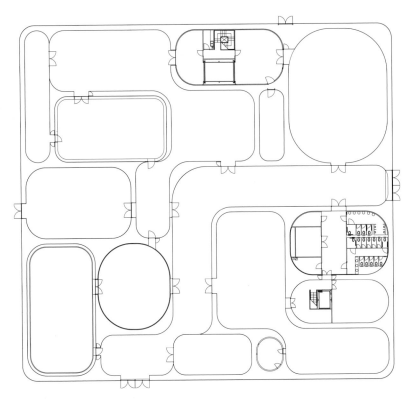

above The climate engineering firm Transsolar designed space for air to flow between the "cellular structures" of the interior and the glass façade that envelops the building. Heat from the glass-blowing studios is redirected through these narrow channels to create a thermal buffer and prevent condensation caused by large temperature differentials.

opposite top Built around three courtyards, each one of the 360 glass panels is approximately 2.5 m (8 ft) wide by 4 m (13.5 ft) high and weighs 600–700 kg (1,300–1,500 lbs). It took expert engineers at Guy Nordenson & Associates to design a system of narrow steel columns (far right) to support the roof structure.

opposite bottom The iron content of the glass was reduced to eradicate the common greenish tint that glass adopts especially when seen from a sharp angle. Thanks to this careful material consideration, the Toledo Pavilion's compacted transparencies break down the perception of inside and outside and contribute a unique element to the landscape.

While curving the glass adds stiffness, the panels are only able to support themselves: they are not load-bearing. The roof is held up by steel beams, which also contain the cable and pipe ducts, allowing the glass surfaces to rise unadorned. The result is an exceptional degree of clarity, but also a veil of disorientation as multiple layers of reflection and refraction from the curved surfaces visually dissolve the boundaries that typically tell the visitor where inside ends and outside begins.

PVB laminate layers sandwiched between the glazing are from the same family of plastics as vinyl, but do not have the same concerns over toxicity. Optically transparent, the material can withstand extended UV radiation and can be tinted with a full spectrum of colors. This version of laminated glazing also incorporates Pilkington's ultra-high-light-transmission, low-iron glass, Optiwhite, giving the walls of the museum an exceptional transparency, like a jewel floating above the grass.

MUSEUM FOLKWANG

CLIENT
Neubau Museum Folkwang
Essen GmbH

ARCHITECT
David Chipperfield Architects

MATERIAL ENGINEER
KonTec Fassadenberatung,
Pazdera AG (façade)

LOCATION
Essen, Germany

COMPLETION
2010

SIZE
16,000 m² / 172,223 ft²

MATERIAL
Structuran recycled-glass ceramic

RELATED MATERIALS
MC# 2721-06, MC# 5163-03

opposite top David Chipperfield Architects designed their addition to the Museum Folkwang with translucent glass panels and courtyards that bring muted light into the interiors and create visual links with the foliage beyond the museum's walls.

opposite bottom Opaque from afar and translucent up close, the museum's fused-glass façade has more in common with architectural ceramic than glazing.

overleaf From a large window, visitors are afforded a unique sightline along the façade of the addition, which was carefully designed to fit into the surrounding urban fabric.

Minimal designs, for all their barely-there appearance, often require maximum attention to craft and execution. As such, a "minimal" structure can be as luxurious to experience as any grand Baroque confection. When materials are reduced to their essence, and their full potential is revealed, what can result is a sensual beauty that would otherwise be overlooked. Such is the case with the addition designed by David Chipperfield Architects for the Museum Folkwang in Essen, Germany. As the glass-clad museum shows, the firm has far from exhausted the creative potential of classic modern materials, namely glass. The structure, with its translucent, alabaster-like surface whose color shifts with the changing light and its windows that sit level with the façade, attests to the extraordinary range of visual possibilities that exist among materials designed to disappear.

Organized into a series of pavilions, courtyards, and covered walkways, the single-story museum displays stunning works based on the collection of Karl Ernst Osthaus, a leading patron of avant-garde art and architecture at the beginning of the twentieth century from the nearby town of Hagen. In 1902, Osthaus founded the Museum Folkwang. Following his death in 1921, the museum continued in the same spirit until the Nazis denounced much of its contents as "degenerate art" and sold off many artworks. A few objects were recovered after the war, and the acquisition of new art resumed, which gradually led to the need for more exhibition space.

Inside, the galleries have a quiet luminosity. Outside, the Structuran recycled-glass panels offer a more durable alternative to traditional translucent glazing, with a unique aesthetic. The slabs are produced by combining multiple chips of recycled float glass, heating them at a very high temperature until they soften, and then bonding them together in the shape of a panel. The surfaces are then ground down to the required dimensions with a polished or a matte finish. Their horizontal placement on the façade more closely resembles stone cladding. The panels are finished at the corners with L-sectioned glass cover strips, further reinforcing the impression of a solid block.

VAKKO FASHION & POWER MEDIA CENTER

CLIENT
Vakko and Power Media

ARCHITECT
REX

MATERIAL ENGINEER
Front Inc. (façade consultant),
Lamglas (manufacturer)

LOCATION
Istanbul, Turkey

COMPLETION
2010

SIZE
5,400 m² / 58,000 ft²

MATERIAL
Slumped-glass panels processed by laying
a sheet of heated material into a press

RELATED MATERIALS
MC# 6148-01, MC# 6663-01, MC# 6910-01

opposite top Ultra-thin glass was "slumped" to make thick X forms in each window. Slumping glass is usually used for decorative effects and rarely at this scale.

opposite bottom The architects dubbed the thin glass covering "Saran Wrap" for the way it clings to the concrete frame.

overleaf, clockwise from top left REX adapted a previous competition entry with the addition of an uncommonly thin glass curtain wall.

Slumping was used here for structural reasons. The very thin curtain wall is reinforced by the truss-like molded glass that braces it for sudden seismic shifts.

REX's design puts transparency and reflection on display not only with slumped curtain walls but also with mirror-clad structures on the ground and roof.

The self-supporting system within the concrete skeleton holds circulation and restrooms, executive offices, and showrooms.

With its dynamic reflective core of slanted boxes and delicate transparent wrapper, the Istanbul headquarters of the Turkish fashion house Vakko and its youth media venture, collectively known as the Power Group, is an architectural tour de force. In little more than a year, New York-based architecture firm REX took the abandoned skeleton of a previously unfinished project and adapted the U-shaped site to fit a multitude of functions: museum, auditorium, library, dining hall, offices, showrooms, even a subterranean radio and television station.

The building consists of two distinct forms: a six-floor tower known as the "Showcase" establishes a central core to the outer concrete "Ring." To provide stability in a region prone to earthquakes, the Showcase is detached so as not to impinge on the structural integrity of the skeleton. Clad in mirrored glass, steel boxes have been stacked at divergent angles to one another, creating a natural series of slopes, which provide a circulation path up through the various communal spaces. From outside, the Showcase's reflective surfaces seem to merge into the sky. The Ring, conversely, consists of floor-to-ceiling window panes slumped with structural Xs to increase strength at the same time as reducing thickness.

The slumping process required to create these uniquely shaped, stronger glass panels needs careful control so that the X does not droop too far (or too little) into the mold, which would reduce rather than enhance the glazing's strength. Each panel is produced by hand in specifically designed molds. The advantage of this innovation is that by slumping a structural X into each pane to increase the glass's strength, the pane's thickness is reduced and the need for perimeter mullions is eliminated. With REX's design, this allows for a play of opacity and transparency that speaks to the twin aspects of Vakko's public image: one focused on the image reflected back onto the consumer, the other suggestive of open access to communication and culture.

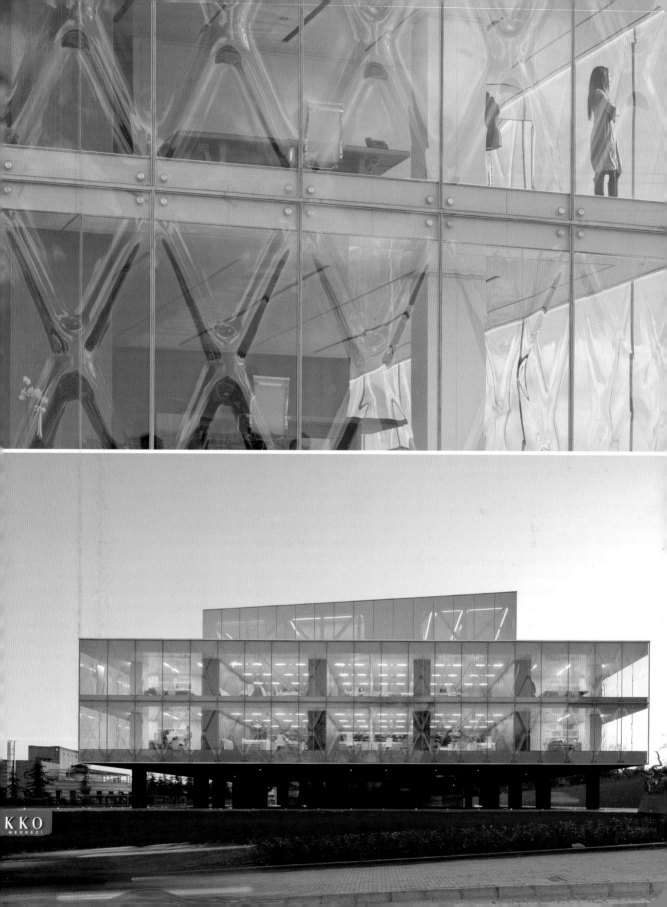

ALTERSWOHNEN DOMAT/EMS

CLIENT
Jürgen Schwarz

ARCHITECT
Dietrich Schwarz Architekten AG

MATERIAL ENGINEER
Dietrich Schwarz Architekten AG

LOCATION
Domat/Ems, Switzerland

COMPLETION
2004

SIZE
148 m² / 1,593 ft² GlassX crystal

MATERIAL
GlassX thermoregulating panels
with phase-change material (PCM)

RELATED MATERIALS
MC# 4756-01, MC# 4756-04,
MC# 5476-02, MC# 6910-03

opposite Situated in Domat/Ems
in the Swiss Alps, this retirement
facility for seniors has been
designed by Schwarz Architekten
with both the climate and the
comfort of the occupants in mind.

The design of this tranquil modernist dwelling in Domat/Ems, a town of fewer than 8,000 inhabitants in Switzerland's Eastern Alps, is based on the enlightened desire to craft an energy-efficient senior residence as an orchestrated blend of positive and negative, lightness and weight. The elongated volume has two faces, in an economical, energy-saving form of construction. The south façade is fully glazed with prismatic glass elements that reflect sunlight in summer while receiving lower-altitude sunshine in winter; the north face is largely closed off to act as a shield.

The exterior is sheathed in glass and locked into an aluminum and timber grid supported by concrete floor slabs. Across the façade, slim vertical rods that serve as balcony railings break up the long expanses of glass and introduce texture into the well-established lexicon of modernism. Rigorous and unobtrusive details give the exterior an air of quietude and grace, in keeping with the setting and the lifestyle of the residents. In practical terms, the dwelling comprises four floors with stairways threading up through each floor's loft-like public spaces from which small apartments, all with their own compact balcony, are accessible.

Like a delicate membrane, the glazing system combines two unexpected materials for architecture: polycarbonate as a twin-wall extruded panel, which is then filled within the carved-out channels with small particles of a phase-change material. This panel is then sandwiched between two exterior layers of glass. The phase-change material effectively equalizes the temperature differences between the exterior and interior spaces, helping to keep the interior warm in winter and cool in summer. It does this by absorbing heat through a change from solid to liquid when warm, and then giving the heat back when the temperature drops. That the phase-change material is also translucent means the glazing can allow light through to the interior space.

top The northern side of the building is sealed from temperature fluctuations, allowing for a more organized airflow.

center left Slowly allowing more heat exchange as it turns to liquid in the sun, GlassX is used to greatest effect in glazing the south façade, which has the most solar exposure.

opposite center right When insulation is required to retain heat, phase-change material (PCM) enters an opaque solid state (shown), which buffers the building from heat loss.

opposite bottom PCM absorbs heat and stores that energy until it reaches 24°C (75°F), at which point the material stabilizes temperature and gradually changes from a solid to a liquid.

above Schwarz Architekten employed 148 m² (1,593 ft²) of PCM on the south-facing façade of the building. By covering their structure in this innovative material the architects have taken an unprecedented step toward adaptive and efficient building design.

NETHERLANDS INSTITUTE FOR SOUND & VISION

CLIENT
Netherlands Institute for Sound and Vision
(Beeld en Geluid)

ARCHITECT
Neutelings Riedijk Architects

MATERIAL ENGINEER
Jaap Drupsteen (façade design) with
Saint-Gobain Sas Glas

LOCATION
Hilversum, The Netherlands

COMPLETION
2006

SIZE
30,000 m² / 322,917 ft²

MATERIAL
Crea-Lite from Saint-Gobain:
individually designed glass with
thermoformed relief elements

RELATED MATERIALS
MC# 6210-01, MC# 6244-01, MC# 6634-01

opposite Neutelings Riedijk Architects worked with artist Jaap Drupsteen to create a structural grammar of squares not only in the vibrating metal plates and etched stained-glass panels but also in the cubic building envelope.

overleaf, clockwise from top left Half of the cube is underground. The upside-down cascade of museum floors can be seen from the outside through the vibrant building envelope.

The artist processed stills from television archives to "translate" the contrast of each image into relief lines that could be etched in the glass.

Drupsteen used software to motion-blur the color of each image, abstracting to provide visual continuity along the façade.

In total 2,100 different-colored high-relief glass panels were manufactured nearby in Eindhoven and carefully lifted into place.

The Netherlands Institute for Sound and Vision, located southeast of Amsterdam in Hilversum, the center of the Dutch television industry, houses one of the largest audiovisual archives in Europe, including more than 750,000 hours of television, radio, music and film, preserving a major part of the Dutch audiovisual heritage. The institute is responsible for keeping the collection in optimal condition, for both present and future use. It also houses a museum, making it a new cultural focal point for the city.

From the outside, the institute reads as a single block, and it is indeed a perfect cube of 50 x 50 x 50 meters (164 x 164 x 164 feet), subdivided into different spaces and sunk half-way into the ground. A lightweight steel frame is sheathed in a spectacular skin of cast-glass panels impregnated with famous images from Dutch television. Through the colored relief of the panels, the structure hints at the contents within, as well as the activities that take place there, giving the building a highly distinctive public face that attracts upwards of a million visitors annually. Unlike the plastic (PVB, or polyvinyl butyrate) interlayer that is printed on for standard graphic glazing, these panels were created through a process that permanently fuses the image into the glass, baking the layer so that it is a durable, UV-resistant and high-quality composite. It also ensures that the image is protected from any dirt or moisture for decades.

YALE UNIVERSITY SCULPTURE BUILDING & GALLERY

CLIENT
Yale University

ARCHITECT
KieranTimberlake

MATERIAL ENGINEER
Atelier Ten (solar modeling), Schuco (shading)

LOCATION
New Haven, Connecticut, USA

COMPLETION
2011

SIZE
4,738 m² / 51,000 ft² (Sculpture Building),
279 m² / 3,000 ft² (Gallery)

MATERIAL
Kalwall panels and Cabot Lumira aerogel

RELATED MATERIALS
MC# 4755-02, MC# 6912-01

opposite In an effort both to bring the building in line with the highest LEED (Leadership in Energy and Environmental Design) standards and to accommodate Yale's Gothic architecture, KieranTimberlake designed contemporary fenestration to mitigate solar gain.

With its Gothic and Colonial Revival structures framing intimate courtyards and gardens, Yale University is among America's most beautiful college campuses. But it also possesses a collection of important modernist structures that offer a rich commentary on contemporary campus aesthetics, including the Beinecke Rare Book and Manuscript Library by Gordon Bunshaft, Ingalls Rink by Eero Saarinen, the Art and Architecture Building by Paul Rudolph, Louis Kahn's Art Gallery and Mellon Center for British Art, and Frank Gehry's Yale Psychiatric Institute, among others.

As part of Yale Tomorrow, a long-range capital campaign for the university, a strategy was put in place to encourage interaction among the visual and performing arts, which included relocating the sculpture department to allow for a new complex within easy proximity to several companion creative facilities and linked to the neighboring New Haven community.

Architects KieranTimberlake responded with a sculpture complex fine-tuned to the specifics of artistic activity, in particular the physical demands of three-dimensional form. Previously a parking lot, the site includes three new buildings: a four-story sculpture department, a one-story storefront gallery, and a four-story parking garage. The gallery and parking structure

left Translucent spandrel windows in the space between the top of the window in one story and the sill of the window in the story above are filled with aerogel, an ultra-lightweight insulating material that is made by replacing the liquid component of a gel with a gas.

opposite top The Sculpture Building and Gallery sit across from a new parking structure, the complex forming part of an initiative both to improve arts facilities and to lower the carbon footprint of the university.

opposite bottom Wrapping around the corner studio at waist level, translucent panels filled with Cabot's Lumira aerogel insulate with high efficiency without becoming a barrier to light.

redefine the block's perimeter, while the Sculpture Building illuminates the core, conceived as a mid-block lantern. The Sculpture Building provides three floors of individual and group studios above a ground floor and basement of classrooms, machine shops, and administrative spaces. The four-story glass structure is enclosed by a high-performance curtain wall that envelops 4.3-meter (14-foot) high studios on the upper floors and workshops, as well as classrooms on the first floor. At night, the façade emits a soft, glowing light, which challenges future built projects to rise to its standing as Connecticut's first building to qualify for a LEED Platinum rating from the US Green Building Council.

Both the translucent glow and the LEED Platinum rating were achieved through the use of aerogel, a super-insulating "solid smoke" material, which has been integrated into the curtain wall. The panels, created by Kalwall, were filled with loose microspheres of the glass foam aerogel that allows for energy-efficient performance with significant light transmission.

BAHÁ'Í TEMPLE OF SOUTH AMERICA

CLIENT
The National Spiritual Assembly of the Bahá'ís of Chile

ARCHITECT
Hariri Pontarini Architects

MATERIAL ENGINEER
Hariri Pontarini Architects, Jeff Goodman Studio, and Simpson Gumpertz & Heger

LOCATION
Santiago, Chile

COMPLETION
Projected 2015

SIZE
2,276 m² / 24,500 ft²

MATERIAL
Slumped panels processed by laying glass rods in a sheet and baking them

RELATED MATERIALS
MC# 5701-02, MC# 6154-01

opposite, clockwise from top left Artist Jeff Goodman worked for years to learn how to lay glass rods on a sheet and bake them to make a uniform 32-mm (1.25-in.) thick cast-glass panel.

A section of water-jet-cut cast-glass panel curves around an aluminum scaffold at Gartner Steel and Glass testing facility in Bavaria.

The architects were inspired by the idea of "structured light" that the thin translucent glass embodies.

Nine translucent "petals" open to the outside world in Hariri Pontarini's adaptation of traditional Bahá'í worship houses.

overleaf Scheduled for completion in 2015, the project is currently under way in Chile.

Set at the foot of the Andes Mountains, in the hills of Peñalolén, Santiago, amid contemplative gardens and reflecting pools, the Bahá'í House of Worship, designed by Canadian-based Hariri Pontarini Architects, will be a luminous gathering place whose essential message is unity: of God, of humanity, and of spiritual enrichment. This theme produced a building defined by three key attributes: a circular plan, an ascendant form, and materials specifically chosen for their ability to capture and respond to light. The overall shape is vegetal, with walls billowing out like sails to suggest movement and passage, an architectural scheme made possible by a steel superstructure set into a concrete foundation able to accommodate seismic activity in the area. Exterior walls clad in glass and interior walls clad in translucent marble rise nearly 30 meters (100 feet) to an oculus, recalling such ancient forms as the Pantheon in Rome and Native American kivas.

Glass and marble are delicate, inflexible materials, so the structural system has to be stable and watertight, while the foundation has to be able to accommodate movement in the earth. In addition, the geometry and curvature of the nine translucent exterior walls make the building complex. The outer surface consists of 3,190 square meters (32,290 square feet) of panels made with an entirely new method of casting glass. To create the flat panel glass preforms, numerous transparent cast-glass rods are heated to soften the material before they are cast together into small slabs. This creates a unique internal structure of transparent sections bounded by translucent boundaries, translating light like no other form. A further slumping process to form these slabs into uniquely curved and angled pieces was essential not only for the creation of the overall shape of the façade but also to comply with the architect's demand for minimal connections between the separate panels. The resulting material surface can withstand the "400 years" for which the structure is designed to stand.

Employing structure as décor is a long-standing modernist principle. Here, the architects have also relied on the way light interacts with the materials as a key expressive component.

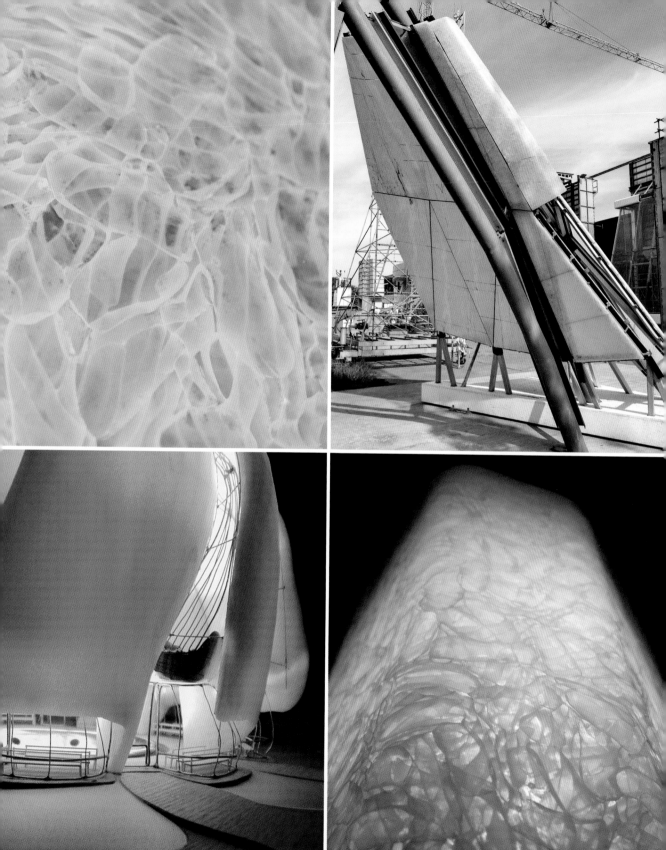

1. **2.**

3. **4.**

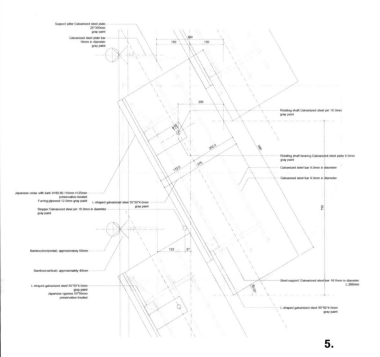

5.

1. Yusuhara is known as a town of "Cha-do," a small thatched pavilion specially built in old times to offer teas and entertain tourists. Even now 13 pavilions remain along the main roads in town. People of Yusuhara are proud of Cha-do as a symbol of their hospitality.

2. Thatch adjusts levels of humidity and insulation, and is also an environmentally friendly material. However, the number of thatched houses has been rapidly decreasing in recent years, which reduces the number of thatching specialists and raises the price of the material. As a result, it causes a vicious circle of making thatching even more difficult. This project started to change this situation.

3. KKAA was asked by the town of Yusuhara to design a three-story hotel. Until then, there had been no cases of using thatch for the exterior of a box-type building. We discussed this a lot with the authorities and obtained permission to apply thatching as "windows" that resolve horizontally, rather than as exterior walls.

4–5. 1m- x 2m-sized thatched unit turned around to ventilate the building naturally.

6-7-8. Installing the thatched unit.

9-10. We designed the detail so that you can see the unit back from the interior, so that the warm and soft touch of the thatching can be further experienced. This is also effective for the thatch to adjust easily to the level of humidity.

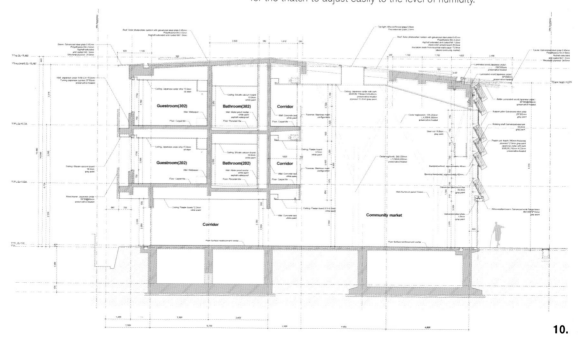

10.

This bench is made of softwood, which is less expensive than hardwoods, yet it is just as durable because it has been treated with heat, pressure, and a chemical called acetic anhydride that vastly reduces the wood's permeability to water and thus its propensity to rot.

CHAPTER 2
ALTERED NATURALS

During the last century, great progress was made in materials technology, but often at the expense of nature. The natural world was to be kept apart, tamed, or improved upon. Synthetic products, interiors and climates assumed we were better than nature, promising a future of minimalist rigor and ascetic cleanliness. Now, advances in medicine and a greater understanding of the natural world mean that we are beginning to realize that our future will likely be better if we work with, rather than against, nature. The simple evolutionary fact is that inferior, less efficient versions of a process gradually die out, leaving us with ever better examples of maximum efficacy and minimal waste.

The natural processes we see around us are the culmination of millions of years of trial and error. In our search for a better understanding of nature, we have become more attuned to its intentions, advantages, and limitations. Biotechnology reveals the infinite possibilities that nature offers, if approached as a harmonious collaboration. Biomimicry has provided a framework for exploring alternative solutions to materials and structures that can support a zero-net-energy architecture by duplicating processes found in nature, yet to truly evolve we need to do more than merely mimic the natural world. Altered Naturals looks at solutions that use natural materials as their source, but work with nature's own processes to improve on them. Initial innovations in this field suggest that we can achieve results better than even the most high-performance human-created materials. It is a future filled with potential.

NATURAL FIBERS

Of course "altering" nature is nothing new in materials—some of the first plastics created at the turn of the twentieth century were made from cotton, wood fibers, and soy. But it is now, with our more complete understanding of nature's processes, that we can not just alter but work with them to reduce energy, cut waste, preserve resources, and improve performance. Examples of innovation that improve on nature's processes include nanocomposite additives from wood fibers or even degraded carrots, which offer degrees of stiffness greater than carbon fiber. Insulation and packaging materials can be made by growing fungi on agricultural waste using no water or sunlight. Such examples take existing natural processes—the rotting of carrots and fungi's ability to grow in the dark without additional water—and work with them to create materials that possess incredible properties while requiring very little energy input.

Working against nature tends to require significant energy, while simply helping it along provides far greater advantages. The example of nanocomposite additives from wood fibers is shown in a product called nanocrystalline cellulose (NCC), in which cellulose, the primary building block of plants, is altered by milling and then hydrolyzing to remove amorphous sections, leaving only the crystalline, high-performance part. This forms a strong but lightweight additive that can be used to strengthen and toughen composites, coatings, fibers and textiles, and also provide biocomposites for tooth and bone repair.

Nanoprocessing enhances natural fibers such as kenaf, flax and jute, giving them improved properties—they contain less water and air (detrimental to high-performance use) and bond better to plastics, making them a viable alternative to glass, carbon and Kevlar fibers. Toyota Motor Corporation in Japan first used kenaf in door trims in 2000 and is working to make all interior parts from plant materials. These developments will allow it to use the fibers in smaller amounts, and in a wider range of places.

One little-mentioned issue with the use of natural fibers, however, is that when they are heated in order to thermoform or injection-mold them with a plastic, they emit the heavy odor of a barn—less than ideal for the workers processing the product. This can be remedied through good ventilation, but to date it has deterred the development of these incredible, grown, strength-possessing fibers.

ENHANCING TIMBER

This trajectory also includes the viable commercialization of acetylation, a process originally patented in the 1930s that increases the strength and durability of timber, making it impervious to the elements and to insects. Acetylation uses vinegar-like compounds to "lock" the cell structure of the wood, stopping the ingress of water and the consequent swelling, as well as its digestion by bugs. This enables fast-growth wood, such as pine, to achieve similar durability to slow-growth exotic woods, such as teak.

BACTERIA

Now that we better understand bacteria, we know that many of them are essential to life and also have incredible problem-solving possibilities. They are one of the building blocks for biopolymer production, used by Metabolix to create Mirel, a seawater-biodegradable plastic that has great engineering applications. Mirel is also used as a potential sealant for concrete, able to "swim down into cracks and secrete a mixture of bacterial glue and calcium carbonate."

Textile-like membranes are now made by harnessing bacteria's ability to deposit tough films when given warm sugary kombucha tea, again with virtually no energy input. These sewable, colorable "fabrics" are being manufactured into clothing, and have other potential textile uses.

Bacteria can also be used to create construction bricks (along with sand, calcium chloride, and urine), whose manufacturing potentially reduces the 1.3 trillion pounds of CO_2 that the production of kiln-fired bricks emits annually. Via the process of microbial-induced calcite precipitation, the bacteria glue the sand together through a chain of chemical reactions, making a brick equivalent in strength and durability to a kiln-fired one.

LOCALIZED RESOURCES

Ecosystems are inherently localized, and by extension biomimicry processes are dependent upon their surrounding conditions to work effectively. Thus, when using natural materials, the preference should be to source them locally, where they are more readily available and will potentially perform more effectively through proximity to the place where they were grown. Atelier Tekuto's "Earth Bricks" use local soils combined with magnesium oxide from either the ocean or land-based mines, offering a lower-impact, more harmonious material solution for construction. The bricks pass Japanese strength requirements for construction (the most stringent in the world), and the manufacturing process is being transferred to other locations globally. Similar processes are being achieved with the use of hemp as a fibrous strengthener in bricks, transforming local waste fibers into a building resource for carbon-negative, high-compressive-strength construction materials.

OVERALL RESOURCES

The question of how to optimally balance local, harvested resources between land use for food and land use for industry and construction has yet to be resolved. The transition from first-stage to third-stage biopolymers exemplifies the issue. The first generation of biopolymers derived from annually harvested crops used food-grade resources such as corn or sugar cane, which negatively affects the availability of food resources and affects food prices. The second generation of biopolymers used either waste materials from harvesting or food production, or non-food-producing crops such as castor beans or rapeseed; a step forward, but still negatively impacting the land available for food growth. The third generation of biopolymers is grown directly from bacteria or seaweed in tanks that can be properly industrialized and does not affect the human food chain. This most recent option allows for a future in which sufficient materials can be grown without having an

impact on our ability to feed humans. This underscores the need to work with nature through industrialized, highly efficient methods that provide the scale needed to compete with today's extensive, and entrenched, material production methods.

Our future on this planet requires a more viable energy balance between what we take and what we use. To achieve this, production and construction need to become vastly more efficient to the extent that they mimic nature, leading to a zero-sum game. For that to occur, the processes that we encounter in nature every day that require no more energy than is supplied by the sun, or other life forces, and leave no waste will need to form the basis for our current energy-intensive processes. It is clear this is possible, for both small-scale consumer products and the built environment.

Capsule Lights from MIO are made with locally sourced wool, a rapidly renewable and biodegradable natural material that designers Jamie Salm and Katherine Wise used to design a light that could be composted at the end of its lifetime.

These trivets are made with cork granulate, a by-product of the wine stopper industry. Every six years cork is harvested from mature trees, which will regrow their bark over the next few years.

KILDEN PERFORMING ARTS CENTRE

CLIENT
TKS IKS

ARCHITECT
ALA Architects

MATERIAL ENGINEER
designtoproduction GmbH
(Wave Wall)

LOCATION
Kristiansand, Norway

COMPLETION
2012

SIZE
16,000 m² / 172,223 ft²

MATERIAL
Digitally modeled and CNC-milled
parametric oak paneling

RELATED MATERIALS
MC# 6919-01

ALA Architects' Kilden Performing Arts Centre in the southern Norwegian city of Kristiansand is exceptional as a physical manifestation of its inspiration—music—and for its elegant, yin/yang delineation of form. Crisp, folded planes of blackened concrete wrap around the building on three sides. Beneath this dark hood is a set of performing arts spaces: a 1,200-seat concert hall, a 700-seat theater, and a stage for experimental theater, all linked by a glass-walled lobby whose bold, rippling ceiling plane seems to project so much glorious sound out across the harbor and surrounding cityscape. Inclined upward from its waterside location at the edge of a pier, this vast, undulating oak plane conveys both drama and restraint. The warm, tactile surface references the region's heritage as a source of timber and conveys a resonance appropriate to a performance space able to accommodate instruments of all kinds.

Kilden is the second most significant cultural building to be completed in Norway during the past decade, following Snøhetta's daring, award-winning design for the Norwegian National Opera and Ballet in 2007, itself the largest cultural building constructed in Norway since the medieval Nidaros Cathedral (dating back to around 1300). While the process of fabricating the dramatic angled façade

left In this detailed parametric model by engineers at Zurich-based designtoproduction, the steel frame that supports the "Wave Wall" is shown in red and the precisely milled secondary beams in white.

opposite Kilden's undulating oak façade cantilevers up to 35 m (115 ft) to hover above the water's edge at its peak.

left In the factory, secondary beams with "seat cuts" milled for precise installation along the cantilevered steel frame ensure consistent 10-mm (0.4-in.) gaps between each piece of oak cladding.

below Wooden ribs attached to steel beams hold the milled oak boards in place.

bottom Structural engineers SJB Kempter Fitze and shipbuilding specialists RisørTrebåtbyggeri helped designtoproduction create a pre-assembly system that allowed the wooden façade elements to be assembled and delivered in panels, ready to be installed on Kilden's steel frame.

opposite top Designtoproduction was commissioned by Norwegian timber contractor Trebyggeriet to coordinate the modeling and fabrication of the 14,309 individual components that comprise the wave.

opposite bottom Lit from inside by Fagerhult lighting, the Kilden Centre emerges from the dark industrial surroundings of the Kristiansand pier to softly reflect the glow across the harbor.

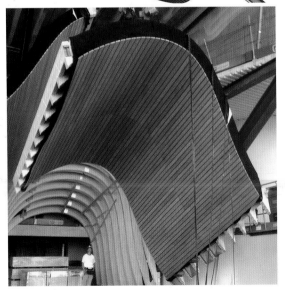

relied on the latest digital modeling of the curved beams and CNC (computer numerical control) milling techniques, all of the connection details were self-positioning, which allowed the wood to find its own best way of settling into the overall structure. Unlike synthetic materials, where processing enables the architect to precisely set the form, naturally grown timber must be worked with to find its best mating with other wood pieces. Much in the way that ancient shipbuilders would laminate cladding onto the main skeleton, the oak laminate panels are secured onto the curved timber beams using "seat cuts" (notches) to ensure a good fit. For Kilden, this was all generated by digital fabrication based on a mathematically precise reconstruction of the architect's model. Indeed, to optimize material procurement, this modeling enabled the reduction of the number of different laminate shapes from 1,700 to a mere 126, showing that many of today's best designs are the combined result of experience, intuition, and technology.

VILLA WELPELOO

CLIENT
Tjibbe Knol and Ingrid Blans

ARCHITECT
Superuse Studios

MATERIAL ENGINEER
None

LOCATION
Enschede, The Netherlands

COMPLETION
2008

SIZE
60 m² / 646 ft²

MATERIAL
Reclaimed wood (skin) and seashells
(moisture regulation)

RELATED MATERIALS
MC# 6685-01, MC# 6700-01

opposite top and middle Discovered a mere 2 km (1.2 mi.) from the building site, steel beams from industrial machinery formerly belonging to a textile mill were reclaimed for the structural frame of the building. The architects devised a process to break down cable reels and allocate them for the outer cladding of the house. Aiming to make as much of the house out of recycled materials as possible, they cut down old billboards for cabinetry.

opposite bottom Heat-treating wood at 150°C (302°F) for twenty-four hours changes its physical properties, making it more resistant to rot and further protecting the exterior of the villa.

overleaf Villa Welpeloo was the architects Jan Jongert and Jeroen Bergsma's first house. Their approach is what they call "recyclicity" or "superuse." Beyond the sustainable benefits, it requires greater flexibility from both the designer and the client.

Villa Welpeloo displays its contribution to twenty-first-century residential design through an exceptional mix of salvaged, repurposed, reused, and, in essence, waste material. While the finished dwelling is its own accomplishment, equally noteworthy is the creative process that led to its completion. The architects began by using GPS and digital mapping capabilities to locate abandoned lots and structures within a 15-kilometer (9-mile) radius of the site that could yield source material. In the end, wooden slats, steel, old signs, and even umbrellas made up more than half of the new construction.

Reclamation of no longer useful materials has seen a boom in popularity in the past decade, providing beautiful flooring and cladding for buildings from timber found in such romantic locations as old stadiums, aged barns, and structures in exotic places. But there is no reason that equally attractive materials cannot be salvaged from less glamorous sources—in this case the wooden slats of disused large cable reels from a nearby factory—while also reducing the shipping needed to bring them to the site. Here, materials collected from a thousand reels were sufficient to clad the entire façade. In addition to other reclaimed or recycled materials used on the structure, seashells were used in the walls for their ability to regulate moisture through the porosity of their surfaces, an effective alternative to synthetic means that shows how well locally sourced and often simple solutions can yield big benefits.

The findings prompted new shapes and construction methods able to incorporate the found materials without sacrificing aesthetics. The result of such customization, even with large quantities of standardized salvage, has been a double hit of environmental benefits—the large volume of recycled materials and the short distances involved to get them to the site have meant a greatly reduced carbon footprint. By embarking on a process that is the reverse of the usual sequence, the villa embodies a way of thinking about building—materials first, then house—that encourages serendipity and the unexpected, as well as preservation. But it also gives architects, builders and clients a chance to examine the true meaning of a house with "local roots."

CORK HOUSE

CLIENT
Maria Helena Ramos and Hernâni Lopes

ARCHITECT
Arquitectos Anónimos

MATERIAL ENGINEER
Ricardo Fonseca (structural consultant),
Amorim Isolamentos S.A. (manufacturer)

LOCATION
Esposende, Portugal

COMPLETION
2007

SIZE
288 m² / 3,100 ft²

MATERIAL
Cork cladding panels

RELATED MATERIALS
MC# 4571-04, MC# 6384-03,
MC# 6841-01

opposite top Arquitectos Anónimos's low budget encouraged them to build a simple structure. Besides the natural cladding the only other prominent design expense was for perforated-aluminum folding shutters.

opposite bottom The architects worked with major cork manufacturer Amorim Isolamentos to showcase cork as a functional cladding and insulating material.

Cork's impermeable, buoyant, and elastic qualities make it especially suitable for wine stoppers, shuttlecocks, and building materials. While not a new material— Marcel Proust is famous for lining his Paris bedroom with sheets of cork to muffle the outside noise—its sustainable and renewable aspects have given it fresh appeal. Found in abundance on the Iberian peninsula, where groves of *Quercus suber* flourish, it provided the Portuguese firm Arquitectos Anónimos with a light, strong, low-cost solution to the construction of a holiday house for a family in the coastal town of Esposende.

Set into a hillside, the dwelling has a silhouette that resembles the kind of house a child might draw – a simple rectangle with a classic gabled roof. But the ingenious use of cork blocks, with their natural resistance to fire and effective thermal insulation, gives the minimalist dwelling a humble, earthy tactility that seems entirely appropriate yet new. By unlocking the material's potential, the architects have transformed its often banal appearance into something heroic. Tall, narrow shutters in perforated aluminum offset the brick's mottled surface and reinforce the overall aesthetic simplicity. Beyond their function as a sunblind and security guard, the shutters' cool reflective surfaces and cast shadows help enliven the façade's flat panels.

Cork clearly demonstrates the larger potential that exists in altering natural materials and processes. It has a multitude of advantages that have been exploited over the years, including its behavior when compressed, which has given it great value as a wine stopper. It is durable, lightweight, and water-resistant, and can be fashioned into panels, fabrics and tiles. Our current manufacturing method for the material, however, has not changed in centuries and involves a delicate balance of harvesting and

opposite Outside Portugal cork is not a common building material although it is most plentiful. If it is to become more widely adopted, engineers, scientists, and growers must learn how to produce higher volumes without exhausting this naturally fecund resource.

below Cork is soft and malleable yet durable enough to cut a clean profile against the sylvan landscape of Esposende in the north of Portugal.

nurturing. Take too much away and the cork tree dies; take too little and the quality is diminished. It is precisely these nuances, so central to nature, that advances in the processing of grown materials seek to overcome. The key is to produce nature-based materials in abundance by using natural processes but with more robust, higher-volume production methods. Otherwise, our use of materials such as cork is strictly rationed, limiting its superb use for such projects as the Cork House.

MENTAL HEALTH INSTITUTE GGZ-NIJMEGEN

CLIENT
Pro Persona

ARCHITECT
BogermanDill with SBH Architecten +
Adviseurs

MATERIAL ENGINEER
Jongeneel Projecten (cladding) and
De Jong's Houtwarenfabriek (fabrication)

LOCATION
Nijmegen, The Netherlands

COMPLETION
2011

SIZE
3,213 m² / 34,584 ft²

MATERIAL
Accoya acetylated wood

RELATED MATERIALS
MC# 4780-08

opposite top Wooden
slats wrap around this
mental health facility,
twisting up to let light into
the interior and lending
a warm appearance to
the building.

opposite bottom
Thanks to the resilient
nature of acetylated
wood Accoya has a
life expectancy of sixty
years with relatively little
maintenance.

**overleaf, clockwise
from top left** The
architects sought
to differentiate the
substructure of coarse
masonry from the
undulating superstructure
of Accoya slats.

Elements of shipbuilding
surface in the altered
naturals category. Accoya
was chosen because it
was exceptionally weather-
resistant, and malleable
enough to be precisely
steam-bent.

Basalt blocks anchor the
hovering slats of the
clinic; between them is
an outdoor space enclosed
by metal mesh (just
visible overleaf).

The idea of health as a complete state of physical, mental and social well-being, rather than merely the absence of disease, challenges architects to think holistically about the forms they give to spaces where a sense of safety, hope and progress is at a premium. This psychiatric institute in Nijmegen, The Netherlands, consisted of several buildings dating back to the early 1960s. In the intervening decades, dramatic advances in treatment were made, leading to the recognition that the complex needed to be razed and rebuilt to more accurately reflect current standards of care.

Amsterdam-based BogermanDill Architecten in cooperation with SBH Architecten were engaged to first draft a master plan for the site, and then focus on the design of individual buildings. The latest, a short-stay clinic, brings together a coarse masonry substructure and an Accoya wood superstructure in a streamlined design that combats the cold, hard-edged stigma often associated with health-care facilities. The building's rounded corners and smooth contours are made possible thanks to material innovations in the steaming, shaping and bending of wood, lending a typically linear material the sinewy quality of a ribbon.

What makes this possible is Accoya wood, the result of acetylated wood technology, by which the internal composition of a softwood is altered to allow it to withstand northern European winters. The process was first developed before the Second World War, but until now has not been sufficiently cost-effective to be used on a large scale for construction and cladding lumber. In brief, acetylation uses acetic anhydride to change the cell structure of the wood to make it impermeable to water and insects, enabling even pine to withstand up to sixty years of exterior exposure. A comparable process to Kebony (see p.82), it is a much less toxic alternative to the current chemical treatments that are used and does not change the color of the timber. These considerations are important as we seek safer, non-toxic, sustainable solutions that deliver better-performing materials for exterior cladding, siding and façades—all situations where reduced maintenance, dimensional stability, and insulation are true advantages.

EARTH BRICKS

CLIENT
Private Residence

ARCHITECT
Atelier Tekuto

MATERIAL ENGINEER
Material testing and development with the help
of Professor Shuichi Matsumura and Kaori
Fujita (Department of Architecture, Graduate
School of Engineering at the University of
Tokyo) and Professor Neoyuki Koshiishi
(School of Creative Science and Engineering
at Waseda University)

LOCATION
Chiba, Japan

COMPLETION
2011

SIZE
47.84 m² / 515 ft²

MATERIAL
Bricks comprised of soil and magnesium oxide

RELATED MATERIALS
MC# 5152-01, MC# 5995-01, MC# 6815-01

opposite The organic
shape of Earth Bricks'
roof and walls is unique in
Chiba, where most houses
are small, rectilinear, and
built with steel frames.

Masonry has been part of Atelier Tekuto's architectural palette for a long time and forms an experimental thread that is woven into the undulating baked-earth dwelling. From the Cell Brick house of 2004 in which steel boxes stacked in a grid pattern transformed the structure into a kind of functional décor, via a luminous, three-story structure composed in different opacities of glass blocks, to the Twin Bricks residence that added ALC (autoclaved lightweight concrete) panels to improve cost-effectiveness, Atelier Tekuto has sought to create varied and striking spaces through the repetition of a single basic unit.

With Earth Bricks, the firm's modular design vocabulary is firmly ensconced in its context, a small urban site that seeks protection and enclosure. Inside, despite the house's tiny footprint, two kinds of space are achieved, proving that even small domains when they are well designed can produce a feeling of expansiveness. The lower level wraps around the inhabitant to provide comfort and security, while the second, sky-lit space seems liberated from terra firma, a level above for setting imagination free.

Tekuto gravitates toward masonry for its "lack of hierarchy between the individual unit and the finished edifice." In this instance, however, he also takes on the quest for an economically and environmentally viable material by asking whether a "new solid structure" could be generated that rises to Japan's exceptionally high structural standards. The solution is to mix magnesium oxide into clay-based soil, an ancient technique found in the pyramids and the Great Wall of China. With this recipe, any soil in the world can be the source of a sustainable construction material, and houses in developing countries where there is a history of natural disasters can be made both safer and more economical.

opposite, clockwise from top left Strong, slender beams made with laminated timber hold up the staircase moving to the second level of the house.

After extensive research and testing, Atelier Tekuto's locally sourced bricks turned out to surpass the Japanese construction standards for masonry, which are the most rigorous in the world.

The built area of the residence is only 47.84 m² (515 ft²), yet the curved walls of the kitchen and bathroom form a welcoming space. According to the architects a total of 2,600 blocks were manufactured from local soil.

below This is the first building in Japan to use masonry made from local soil and magnesium oxide. Thin vented windows in the back of the cocoon-like structure help to regulate the climate inside the house.

The use of magnesium oxide as the binder for the bricks follows a series of other projects that have used this ubiquitous, food-safe chemical for construction. The magnesium mineral, once mixed with the local clay, absorbs carbon dioxide from the air to form magnesium carbonate and solidifies the block, making it more like stone. This is a similar process to some of the latest, more sustainable concrete formulations that replace calcium carbonate with magnesium oxide. The advantage of the magnesium is that the bricks get stronger the longer that they are left out, progressively strengthening even when they are part of the building.

ONDA RESTAURANT

CLIENT
Private Owners

ARCHITECT
Alliance Arkitekter and MAPT

LOCATION
Oslo, Norway

COMPLETION
2011

SIZE
1,250 m² / 13,455 ft²

MATERIAL
Kebony-treated eastern pine

RELATED MATERIALS
MC# 5606-01, MC# 6929-01

opposite Alliance Arkitekter and MAPT designed the Onda Restaurant following the structural logic of boat-hull construction, while respecting Norway's heritage of wood craftsmanship.

overleaf, clockwise from top left The newest building on the Tingvalla pier in Aker Brygge, Onda has a striking roofline that visually anchors it to the boardwalk and will gradually take on a silver-gray patina.

Metal, glass, and wood meet in a design pared down to its elegant essence. The intrinsic qualities of glass are used to maximum degree, allowing guests panoramic views while dining.

The hardy roof material is made by Kebony, a Norwegian company that treats softwood with heat and bio-alcohol. Kebonized wood is 50 percent less likely to splinter and decay, meaning reduced maintenance costs.

The restaurant's palette shifts between the exterior's rustic, patinated texture and the minimal refinement of the interior.

In a city accustomed to long winter twilights and summer days seemingly without night, a restaurant design that emphasizes both warmth and transparency seems especially inviting and apt. Onda Restaurant, Spanish for "wave," sits on the Tingvalla pier in Aker Brygge, Oslo, a modern section of the city that was previously an old shipyard and has now been redeveloped into a lively waterfront district of bars, restaurants, and shopping. Conceived by Norwegian Alliance Arkitekter and Danish architects MAPT, the low, sleek, curvaceous structure exemplifies the recent tendency by architects to merge structure and surface into fluid, organic forms that offer a sensual response to modernism's penchant for the grid.

The seafood brasserie's Kebony-clad roof respects Norway's tradition of building sustainably with wood as well as the neighborhood's heritage, through a sloping form that offers the glass curtain walls a protective hood, much like the overturned hull of a boat. The overall elliptical shape of the restaurant is served by locating the culinary functions inside a central core so that light enters the space from all sides. The underside of the roof is clad in elegant strips of ash that direct the gaze down toward panoramic views of the pier, the city, and the surrounding waters of the fjord.

Though wood is widely used for construction in Scandinavia, many indigenous species do not easily withstand the region's harsh climate, necessitating coatings, treatments, and painting that obscure the natural beauty of the material. The architects' use of a local wood that has been "Kebonized" overcomes this challenge: Kebony wood has undergone a non-toxic treatment involving soaking the timber in furfuryl alcohol, a waste byproduct of sugar cane. No special handling or precautions are needed to deal with waste from this wood, unlike chemical treatments such as chromated copper arsenate, which is now banned for most uses in the USA and the EU, or alkaline copper quaternary compounds. As such, it can be disposed of just like any untreated wood. This process, known as furfurylation, gives the wood a darker color, so that pine resembles teak, ipé, mahogany, and other tropical hardwoods, and makes it similarly durable and resilient.

STADTHAUS, MURRAY GROVE

CLIENT
Telford Homes / Metropolitan Housing Trust

ARCHITECT
Waugh Thistleton Architects

MATERIAL ENGINEER
Matthew Wells with Techniker Engineers and
Karl Heinz Weiss, KLH (manufacturer)

LOCATION
London, UK

COMPLETION
2009

SIZE
2,694 m² / 29,000 ft²

MATERIAL
Prefabricated cross-laminated timber (CLT)
walls and floors

RELATED MATERIALS
MC# 5842-02, MC# 6216-08, MC# 6970-03

opposite Cross-laminated timber (CLT) is a highly engineered building material from a renewable resource. The wooden wall elements form the structural core, and also absorb carbon, helping to compensate for emissions.

overleaf, clockwise from top left The CLT panels were built as large as possible while being easily transportable. At most they weighed 18 tonnes each.

Although it may be difficult to discern on seeing the final building, Stadthaus is, at nine floors and 29 m (95 ft) high, one of the tallest timber-framed structures in the world.

KLH's proprietary installation system enabled structural engineers at Techniker to design the structure of the walls, stairs and lift cores (shown) such that it bears all vertical loads and resists lateral stresses.

The architectural form most emblematic of modern urban living is the apartment building. And the materials most commonly associated with that form are concrete, glass, and steel. With the widely acknowledged adverse effects of carbon emissions on global warming, architects have been looking at a variety of strategies to mitigate the negative effects of both material manufacturing and the construction process, by experimenting with new sustainable options while reevaluating less conventional materials. Stadthaus makes a case for timber as a viable alternative, especially prefabricated cross-laminated timber panels. Timber is not only replenishable but it absorbs and stores carbon, even after it has been cut, helping to offset hazardous emissions. The disadvantages of timber are its lack of sound absorption and need for fire protection, both of which architects Waugh Thistleton, structural engineers Techniker, and timber panel manufacturer KLH were able to overcome in the design and construction of Stadthaus. This is the first high-density housing building to be made from prefabricated cross-laminated timber panels, winning over the Metropolitan Housing Authority, which commissioned the building for the London Borough of Hackney. The result is the tallest modern timber structure in the world: nine floors containing twenty-nine dwellings of social housing and private sale units, all of which were snapped up on the first day.

Much in the way that the digital fabrication of the oak-paneled façade of the Kilden Performing Arts Centre (see pp. 62–65) has taken the craftsmanship of wood construction to a new level, modeling of the stresses within multistory buildings is now enabling the use of timber as an alternative to steel in structural elements. Essential to this is the full understanding of the properties of the wood and treating the construction as a whole rather than as individual parts, which often results in bracing beams across specific spans to ensure overall rigidity. The advances in glue-laminated timber, or glulam, and cross-laminated timber panels (better glues, better geometries) have enabled greater strength, and the digital control of cutting and joining ensures the greatest strength from these timbers. In addition, the cross-lamination gives sound control three times that of conventional buildings.

PAVILION HERMÈS FOR MILAN DESIGN WEEK

CLIENT
Hermès France

ARCHITECT
Shigeru Ban Architects / Jean de Gastines
Architectes

MATERIAL ENGINEER
None

LOCATION
Milan, Italy

COMPLETION
2011

SIZE
214 m² / 2,303 ft²

MATERIAL
Recycled paper tubes

RELATED MATERIALS
MC# 5518-01, MC# 6241-01, MC# 6560-05,
MC# 6589-02, MC# 6842-01

opposite Shigeru Ban worked with colleague Jean de Gastines, with whom he designed the Centre Pompidou-Metz, including its intricate joinery. Here the objective was to create a "nomadic" exhibition structure that could be reassembled in different shapes according to the site condition.

With construction techniques that defy the idea of paper as an ephemeral material, and an elegant, caramel-colored palette, this pavilion for the French luxury brand Hermès exemplifies the work of one of Japanese architecture's most captivating practitioners: Shigeru Ban. Designed as a temporary structure to celebrate and showcase the revival of La Maison, Hermès's product line for the home, at the annual Salone del Mobile in Milan, the rigorously simple, handsomely crafted space reinforces key aspects of the saddler's signature brand traits: inspiration drawn from unsuspecting places and able, when married to exacting craftsmanship, to yield something truly special.

What is exciting about Hermès's move into home furnishings is the restoration of Jean-Michel Frank's furniture designs from the 1920s. Frank was known for incorporating refined materials—cerused (or limed) oak, leather, parchment, shagreen—into his work, and he initiated a collaboration with the leather goods company to provide upholstery for his chairs and tables. Decades later, the selection of an architect recognized for his uniquely sensitive response to a single material, albeit the more humble paper tube, has clear parallels. The alliance with Shigeru Ban also stretches the associations for the brand into new areas less common to the luxury realm, most notably the architect's concern for sustainable development.

In his use of paper for the pavilion, Shigeru Ban again blurs the boundaries between paper and composite materials. The cylindrical geometry of the beams provides considerable engineering strength, but it is the fibrous form of the paper and the bonding agent holding these fibers together that really give the material its value. Ban's decision to keep the paper tubes "standard" by using existing forms discarded from textile factories and paper mills and simply coating or painting them to improve weathering enables these forms to be sourced globally for little cost. While Ban gravitates toward open air and temporary structures, increasingly the response to his work suggests that the short-lived will be around and preserved for years to come.

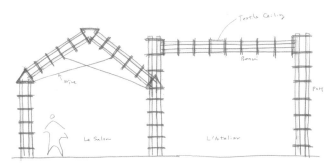

left A birch support beam runs down the top ridge of the pavilion's roof. The pavilion is divided into two semi-nomadic spaces titled here "Le Salon" and "L'Atelier."

below The pavilion heralded Hermès's return to the world of furniture in one of its cultural centers, Milan, where Ban's measured use of materials common to the textile industry made a striking space.

opposite Spirally bound paper tubes used for such humdrum industrial activities as storing textiles are also highly engineered products that can be used in architecture, in part because of paper's natural fibrous structure.

Completion

Installation

Structure

Rationalisation

3D-printed fairings (coverings for a prosthetic leg), offered by Bespoke Innovations in San Francisco, can be coupled with chrome, nylon, carbon fiber, and a range of composites.

CHAPTER 3
HIGH-PERFORMANCE COMPOSITES

Where single material classes such as metals, plastics, or glasses reach the limits of their performance, composite materials take over. Synergistically taking the advantageous parts of two different materials and combining them to give better overall performance, composites have long offered properties unachievable from single materials alone. They are already widely used in architecture, including synthetic versions such as glass-fiber-reinforced plastics (GRPs) and organic alternatives such as glulam (glued laminated timber) beams; MDF and particleboard are basic composites. But this chapter is most interested in advanced composites: those that utilize accurate and fine-scale control of the constituent parts to eke out even greater gains from each individual material. The ultimate goal in this pursuit is one offered, though not yet fully realized, by nanotechnology—that of nanostructured or molecular control of the construction of materials. In this way we can imagine that we will be able to see the often unimaginably strong, lightweight, impact- and heat-resistant complex materials achieved by nature.

DIFFERENT FIBER FORMS AND TYPES IN COMPOSITES

When considering what shape of additive to incorporate into a composite, the hierarchy of strengthening goes from the addition of rounded particles, to short fibers, to long fibers, to continuous-length filaments that run the length of the part, to woven fabrics. Each successive transition of fiber type—from particle to fiber to filament to fabric—leads to higher stiffness, better strength. The strongest composites incorporate woven fabrics of carbon fiber. Given that we are always trying to push our materials to greater limits, what can be done to take this further? In engineering terms—triangles and cylinders.

Triaxial braiding of fibers (60-degree angles between yarns) improves overall strength by reducing weak strength directions (typically at 45 degrees to any line for woven fabric composites). Beyond skis and racing yachts, these have been used to strengthen radio telescope discs and concrete beams in construction (wrapped around the outside), where strength in all directions is essential. Innovations such as the Isotruss use the concept of triangles as inherently strong shapes and combine them in carbon-fiber composite structures to form incredibly stiff tubes for such applications as bicycle frames. This structure has also been posited for use in the construction of antenna poles and towers, as well as in home building. Using a similar truss-type architecture for tubes, Exogrid uses machined-out exoskeleton frames that have carbon-fiber fabric bladders blown into them to fill out the holes and create uniquely 'bi-component' parts for bicycle frames, ski poles, baseball bats, spinnaker poles, and aerospace actuator rods.

Isotruss Manufacturing's three-dimensional truss system weaves composite fibers to create an open lattice structure, which is wrapped with Kevlar and heated until rigid.

High-performance composites are really only as good as the strengthening fibers or fabrics they contain. Well-known examples in the synthetic realm are carbon fiber and Kevlar, but there are significant differences between these (and others) that will limit their use to specific applications.

Carbon fiber and glass fiber are predominantly chosen for their stiffness and tensile strength, and used in parts that require bending or pulling strength such as for spans, tensile architecture, and bicycle frames.

Kevlar, which is an aramid, as well as Dyneema and Spectra, which are ultra-high-molecular-weight polyethylene, have good tensile strength but also superior energy absorption, meaning they are suitable for impact resistance, such as for armor and cut-resistant fabrics. Carbon fiber is not good for bulletproof vests because it is brittle and shatters too easily—Kevlar or Spectra absorb the energy of the bullet without breaking.

Natural fibers such as flax, jute, and wood offer a chance to reduce impact through lower carbon footprint but can also give low weight and, with some enhancements, tensile strengths that rival their synthetic counterparts.

NATURAL FIBERS

As an alternative to synthetic solutions, there have been attempts to create 100 percent natural-based fiber-reinforced advanced composites. Biotex Flax/PLA comprises a woven sheet of flax fiber (three different weave constructions are available) and a PLA (polylactic acid, a corn-based plastic) resin. Currently, commercial applications include consumer products such as snowboards, with parts for use in Land Rover structural sections now being developed. Flax fibers are currently the best strengtheners in the natural fiber world, having tensile strength-to-weight ratios close to that of glass fiber. In order to achieve suitability as construction materials, however, they need to be used with more fire-retardant resins. PLA does not pass standard fire tests for architectural applications, but tests are being undertaken with thermoset furan (an organic compound) resins derived from biomass waste that give the composites a UL 94 V0 level, one of the most stringent fire-retardancy ratings for home appliances and devices.

Some other developments in natural fibers have included nanostructured cellulose and degraded carrot fibers, which are challenging the tensile strengths of even carbon fiber, and these are discussed at greater length in the "Altered Naturals" section of this book.

POLYMER-BASED COMPOSITES

Although composites tend to be one material strengthened by the incorporation of another, some of the newer polymer-based composites use the same material (albeit in a slightly different state) as both matrix and fiber. Self-reinforced plastics (SRPs) such as self-reinforced polypropylene (SRPP) use higher-strength fibers of polypropylene (PP) combined with a more flexible PP matrix. This allows excellent bonding between the two materials (one of the key needs) and also recyclability, which is one of the major concerns over the proliferation of this class of material. Recent applications have included suitcase shells, alternatives to carbon fiber in high-performance motor racing shells such as for NASCAR (stock car), and protective headgear. Dow's recent use of a polyolefin-based architectural fabric strengthened by a similar plastic-type polyethylene terephthalate (PET) for the London 2012 Olympics enables the fabric to be more easily recycled after use (the two plastics do not need to be separated before melting down). The polyolefin gives the weather protection; the PET gives the tensile strength.

CEMENT-BASED

While most standard concrete has not changed much in the last 200 years since the development of Portland cement, the way in which we have tried to improve this material for higher-performance applications has led to formulations and properties that make it closer to an advanced composite than a basic construction material. "High-performance concretes" (HPCs) and now "ultra-high-performance concretes" (UHPCs) combine Portland cement, silica fume, quartz flour, fine silica sand, water, and fine steel or organic fibers. They comprise an optimized gradation of granular constituents, a water-to-cementitious materials ratio less than 0.25, and a high percentage of discontinuous internal fiber reinforcement.

The first bridge made from UHPC was created in 2002 in France, with various other projects since, including the first road bridge in the USA in Iowa in 2006. It is likely that more spans and structures that require light weight, stiffness, and a degree of ductility (untypical of regular concrete, which is very brittle) will use these types of composites; as of early 2012, eighteen bridges in the USA and Canada had been constructed with this material. Advances are going to come in the area of greater shape freedom: the concrete-based material Ductal from LaFarge is a specific version of UHPC that has been used to create dramatically sculptural concrete structures with molded thinner form factors and more organic shapes. This "concrete composite" has significantly higher tensile and flexural strength than regular concrete, and so can be used in these newer thin-form section applications, but to do this requires very close control (on the nanostructural level) of the composite composition, particulate size and distribution—a far cry from the basic mixing of standard concrete. This takes concrete from its traditional role as a load-bearing massive material into the realms of tensile and flexural materials such as standard glass-fiber-reinforced composites and even metals, and opens up completely new thinking on what concrete is.

A NOTE ON RECYCLABILITY

A long-held concern about the move toward composite materials—those that use two or more distinctly different constituents to create a synergistically higher-performance material—is that once you put the parts together, you cannot easily pull them apart again at their end of life. The better a composite is made, the better the resin and fibers are bonded and thus the harder they are to separate. To date, there have been virtually no methods to recycle composites effectively. Add to this that most current advanced GRP

Composite materials paired with Siemens' IntegralBlade design process allow an entire wind-turbine blade to be produced without any bonded joints in one mold.

composites used in architecture use *thermoset* polymers, which cannot be re-melted once made (they just char when heated sufficiently), and you have a major challenge. There are some innovations in this area that look at how the resin (glue) can be "activated" by specific conditions, such as certain wavelengths of light, certain vibration frequencies, or heat and pressure conditions, to release their fibers and be effectively separated. This is also being investigated with glues for laminates that can be pulled apart under specific conditions. It is a small start, but as Boeing has said on its 787 Dreamliner, which is more than 50 percent composite materials, "by the time it is time to retire the aircraft we will be able to recycle more of it than an aluminum one."

It is clear that the range of material combinations that is possible in the field of advanced composites challenges our understanding of material types, with modern concretes and plastics already more composite than single material. The future lies in how well we can control these combinations, potentially using new fabrication techniques such as additive manufacturing or knitting to give the precise interlayering and microstructural control that is common in natural composites that we aim to mimic. Then, of course, once we have created these intricate masterpieces of function and performance, how do we repurpose them for a second life?

COCOON_FS PAVILION

CLIENT
PlanktonTech with the Alfred Wegener
Institut, Bremerhaven

ARCHITECT
Pohl Architekten

MATERIAL ENGINEER
Pohl Architekten, Fiber Tech
(composite shell)

LOCATION
Jena, Germany
(plus sites around the world)

COMPLETION
2010

SIZE
10 m² / 107 ft²
750 kg / 1,650 lbs

MATERIAL
Fiber-reinforced polymer (FRP) shell

RELATED MATERIALS
MC# 4896-02, MC# 5323-04, MC# 6428-01

opposite top Pohl
Architekten pressed
fiber-reinforced-polymer
sheets into CNC-milled
molds before heating
them. Fifteen unique base
modules were designed
and a total of 220 were
manufactured.

opposite bottom
Backlit panels show
visible variations in color,
which correspond to the
distribution of material
throughout the shell in
relation to compressive
and tensile forces.

overleaf Designers
generated Voronoi
diagrams with software
and modeled the paths of
stress throughout the shell
to use the least material
possible. The panels
interlock to create an
earthquake-resistant
self-supporting structure.

In an age when it seems that virtually everything has shrunk, the Cocoon_FS Pavilion accomplishes the reverse. This luminous, lightweight structure designed for PlanktonTech by Pohl Architekten invites visitors inside phytoplankton: microscopic organisms that are the first link in the ocean's food chain. The term derives from the Greek *phyto* (plant) and *plankton* (wandering or drifting). Phytoplankton are generally single-celled organisms, which take extraordinarily diverse forms and are often bioluminescent. The Cocoon, through its complex organization of spines, ribs, ridges, and pores, mimics the algae's cell wall in order to acquaint visitors with innovations in lightweight composite structures.

To design the mobile pavilion, researchers at PlanktonTech first transferred the richly patterned shells of the plankton to a computerized 3D model. The models were then analyzed and interpreted as an architectural design. From fifteen base shapes 220 modules were made that fit seamlessly together. During the manufacturing process, the panels were "laid up" into a mold that combined strengthening fibers with an epoxy glue to bond them together, so that each leaf-like panel of fiber-reinforced polymer fastens to the next to achieve a super-strong, self-supporting dome.

In much the same way that high-performance racing yacht hulls are produced, the individual panels provide both structure and skin for the Cocoon. As glass-fiber composites offer a better strength-to-weight ratio than almost any other material, the panels are also incredibly light, enabling the temporary, 3-meter (10-foot) tall pavilion to weigh a mere 750 kilos (1,650 pounds), half the weight of a Mini Cooper.

The Cocoon refers to its marine origins through the use of a special epoxy resin that makes it watertight as well as translucent. Light enters during the day and, akin to its bioluminescent source, the pavilion emits a soft glow at night when lit from within. By translating sea life into built form, the design magnifies the research efforts of PlanktonTech and reveals how our appreciation of biology has evolved from remote scientific specimens to innovative architectural solutions worthy of aesthetic contemplation.

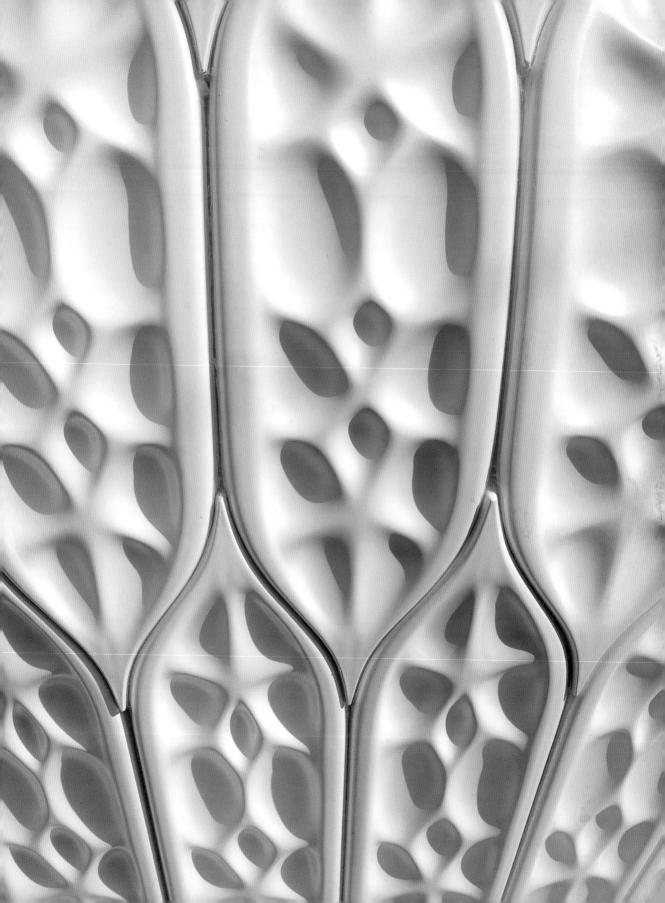

"MODULAR FABRICATION" STAND

CLIENT
Premier Composite Technologies

ARCHITECT
UNStudio

MATERIAL ENGINEER
Premier Composite Technologies

LOCATION
London, UK

COMPLETION
2011

SIZE
50 m² / 538 ft²

MATERIAL
Modules molded from carbon fiber and epoxy resin combined with a structural foam

RELATED MATERIALS
MC# 2492-03, MC# 6733-01

opposite top The modular system comprises jointed components strong and lightweight enough to be taken apart, shipped, and rearranged according to the exhibitor's needs.

opposite bottom Cantilevered over the open space on the floor, the modules include LEDs and touch screens installed in the polyurethane core.

overleaf An early rendering shows bonded joints that were not needed in the final structure—a testament to the iterative design process between the architects and the manufacturer.

UNStudio, the Dutch architectural practice whose projects range from the National Stadium Japan in Tokyo to a museum for the luxury automaker Mercedes-Benz in Stuttgart, Germany, also has a flair for designing exhibitions. Their collaboration with Premier Composite Technologies on a trade show display that showcases the benefits of designing with advanced composite materials over more traditional materials, such as steel and concrete, won a Blueprint Award for Best Stand at 100% Design London 2011.

The design, entitled "Modular Fabrication," transforms the repetition of a single, elbow-shaped module into a meandering track of hexagonal forms that might logically resolve into a honeycomb pattern. Instead, the open-ended configuration suggests a myriad of new spatial arrangements and variations, a key benefit of modular design.

But the stand goes a step further, bridging the gap between architecture and event display through an intriguing combination of high-performance composites and electronic componentry. The exterior is an engineered blend of carbon fiber and glass fiber bonded with an epoxy resin—the carbon provides superior stiffness yet is lightweight, while the glass reduces the overall cost. The core of the hollow square structure is filled with a rigid polyurethane foam, which increases overall strength and improves impact resistance without significantly increasing the weight. The process of filling these hollow sections by blowing expanding foam into the core is typically used in rail and marine applications to ensure that heavy impact does not compromise the shell.

The stand's dramatic scale and linear configuration ingeniously focus the visitor's attention toward small screens embedded in the ends of select modules. The eye travels along the frame to arrive at monitors that offer advanced technological information to visitors, reinforcing the potential for both customized structural configurations and messaging able to surprise and impress multiple visitors.

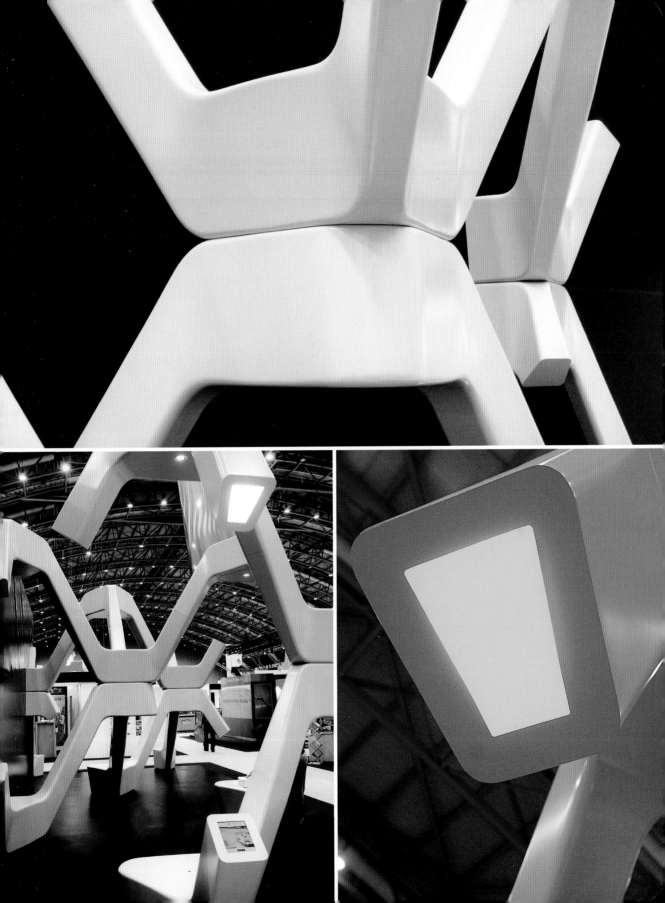

ERICK VAN EGERAAT OFFICE TOWER

CLIENT
Consortium Mahler4

ARCHITECT
Designed by Erick van Egeraat

MATERIAL ENGINEER
Designed by Erick van Egeraat
with Poly Products (manufacturer)

LOCATION
Amsterdam, The Netherlands

COMPLETION
2009

SIZE
33,500 m² / 360,590 ft²

MATERIAL
Gravel-FRP-foam-glass panel

RELATED MATERIALS
MC# 2492-04, MC# 6138-02, MC# 6524-02

opposite The tower features a composite "boulder" above a filigreed glass volume that lets light enter deep into lower floors.

overleaf left The positions of printed elements in the building's lower section were adjusted to track the sun's path across the sky, eliminating the need for sun screens.

overleaf right Erick van Egeraat originally intended to use serpentine marble but, weighing 2,800 kg/m² (570 lb/ft²), it was too heavy for the steel frame. Instead, he turned to Poly Products' Composite Relief System (CRS), which weighed 30 kg/m² (6 lb/ft²).

Amsterdam, like so many cities, keeps pushing at its edges, breaking ground on cutting-edge architecture as it celebrates its historic treasures. Influenced by such models as La Défense in Paris and Canary Wharf in London, Zuidas ("South Axis") is a large new business district south of Amsterdam along the A10 motorway, the ring road that encircles the Dutch capital. The 270-hectare (670-acre) development is knit into Europe's high-speed rail system and the Dutch public transport network, and offers a lively mix of offices, housing, retail, and public spaces designed by nine international architects, all contributing to a compelling ensemble of metropolitan scale.

Within this, Erick van Egeraat's Mahler4 office tower rises like an unearthed crystal, its surface shifting between tones of mica, platinum, and anthracite. Deliberately misaligned facets shimmy up the façade in a highly distinctive dance of tactile surfaces. The stacked block structure evolves counter to the presumed order, from airy below to dense above, as the building's layered sections reveal their own character and tenant needs. The lower, transparent level allows light to penetrate the interior. The uppermost section emphasizes sweeping views. The center transitional portion bridges the unadorned and printed glass components with aluminum panels.

Though giving the appearance of massive weight and the solidity of rock, the façade on the upper section of the tower is constructed from lightweight composite panels that are one-third the density of typical stone. This saves weight, enabling easier and less complicated installation, while still delivering a life expectancy of sixty to a hundred years. To give the composite panels their rock-like appearance, molds were created with a random "rocky" surface. Next a thin layer of granite chips was laid down before the molds were filled with a binding layer of foam-glass granules and resin, followed by a stiff polyester-laminate layer that acts as the back panel to the façade. The panels are then cut to size with a water jet (almost none of the hundreds of panels are identical), and perforated with bolt holes that can be used to secure them to the structure.

HALLEY VI RESEARCH STATION

CLIENT
The British Antarctic Survey

ARCHITECT
Hugh Broughton Architects

MATERIAL ENGINEER
Billings Design Associates (cladding specialist)
and MMS Technology (fabrication)

LOCATION
Brunt Ice Shelf, Antarctica

COMPLETION
2013

SIZE
2,000 m² / 21,528 ft²

MATERIAL
Glass-reinforced plastic (GRP)
insulated panels

RELATED MATERIALS
MC# 0426-02, MC# 5835-01, MC# 6690-01

opposite top Halley VI
Research Center, at the top
of the Greenland ice cap, is
3,225 m (10,580 ft) above sea
level and 400 km (250 mi.)
from the nearest point on land.
Temperatures range from −5 to
−55°C (23 to −67°F) and snow
levels rise annually by a meter
(39 in.) or more.

opposite bottom The
facility is built with highly
insulated glass-fiber-reinforced
(GRP) composite cladding and
integrated photovoltaic arrays.

I magine. You live on the coldest continent on earth, which is also as arid as the desert. Three months of the year is spent in twenty-four-hour darkness and the nearest habitation is an entire continent away in Cape Town, South Africa. How do you survive in such unforgiving conditions? The answer is Halley VI, the newest version of the British Halley Research Station located in Antarctica on the Brunt Ice Shelf.

Ice shelves are important indicators of climate change, enabling scientists to study such things as the earth's magnetic field and atmosphere. In fact, the thinning of the ozone layer was first spotted by Halley scientists in 1985. But for Hugh Broughton Architects, designing the station, and getting it built, required almost as much ingenuity and tenacity as did survival for an Ice Age ancestor. Nine years and $40 million after the small firm won the commission, everything the station needs to function technically, practically, and socially has been configured into 2,000 square meters (21,500 square feet), and every millimeter exists for a reason.

The first five Halley stations were either engulfed by snow or floated away on icebergs. To solve this, Halley VI consists of eight modules strung together in a line and joined with flexible connectors like railway cars. The pods are raised on hydraulic legs that sit on skis. When their position becomes vulnerable, each pod can be lowered and slid to a new site, making this the first fully relocatable station.

In the most recent design, plywood-based SIP (structural insulated panels) used for the aerodynamic shell—at temperatures of −50°C (−58°F) even timber acts as a "cold bridge" into the station interior—have been eclipsed by glass-fiber-reinforced composite panels that incorporate internal insulation specially developed for the station. The most challenging aspect of producing the shell

this page The largest, central module forms the social hub of the base, which is meant for year-round research in both atmospheric and snow chemistry. The interiors were designed in part by Joyce & Reddington in the UK.

opposite The design team added aluminum trihydrate so that the cladding gives off water vapor in a fire. Prefabricated modules were delivered to the building site on truck beds, bolted together, and installed on hydraulic legs that rise in response to snow levels.

panels is their superior fire-retardant requirement. This was met by adding a mineral filler (aluminum trihydrate) to the resin, which had the effect of slowing down the pouring of the resin into the molds used to create the panel shapes. The large, 10.4- x 3.3-meter (3.2- x 1-foot) panels initially suffered from an inadequate mixing of glass fiber and epoxy, causing them to crack in the extreme temperatures. The answer was to further slow down the pouring process to ensure that everything mixed well.

This challenge highlights the almost craftsman-like approach that much composite production requires, especially given the variables and types of materials that must work together to ensure a high-performance product.

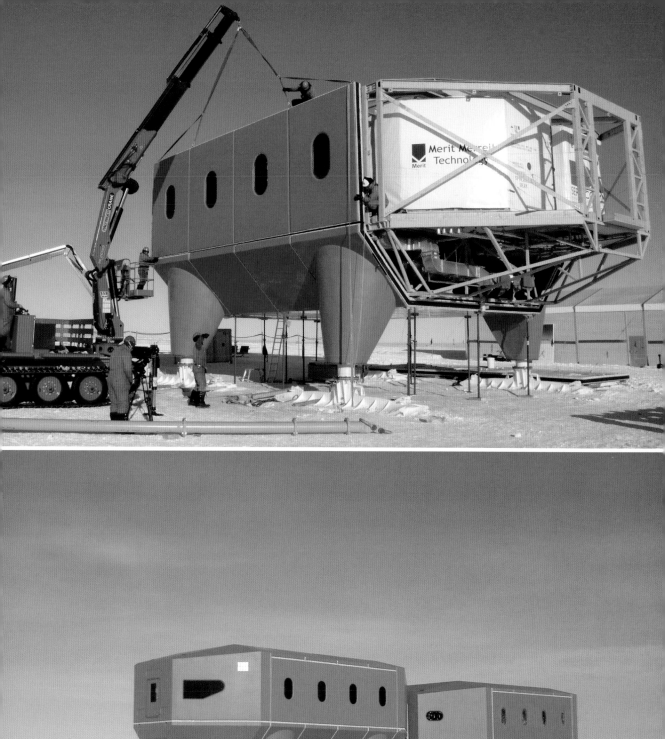

[C]SPACE PAVILION

CLIENT
Architectural Association,
Design Research Laboratory

ARCHITECT
Alan Dempsey and Alvin Huang

MATERIAL ENGINEER
AKT II (structural engineers)

LOCATION
London, UK

COMPLETION
2008

SIZE
100 m² / 1,076 ft²

MATERIAL
FibreC concrete-fiber composite

RELATED MATERIALS
MC# 5232-01, MC# 6621-02,
MC# 6847-02

opposite Spanning 12 m
(39 ft) across a corner of
Bedford Square in London,
this temporary pavilion was the
product of a unique collaboration
between members of the
academy and specialists in
both non-linear structural
analysis and composite
manufacturing processes.

To honor the tenth anniversary of the Architectural Association's Design Research Laboratory (DRL), Alan Dempsey and Alvin Huang conceived of the [C]SPACE Pavilion, an arresting study in simplicity whose seemingly elemental shape reveals itself to be a thoughtful composition of curving dynamism. The fluid, semi-open form is made with fibreC, a glass-fiber-reinforced concrete paneling produced by Rieder, an Austrian supplier of innovative cladding materials. Against the elegant rhythms of a Georgian-era London square, the infinity-like composition wraps into a single-gesture skin, structure, floor, roof, and furniture. The lightness of the moiré mesh appears like a giant hood momentarily inflated by a breeze.

The ability to give concrete, a rigid, obdurate material, the fluid nature of fabric is an impressive feat, emphasizing the values of exploration and possibility that are intrinsic to the DRL. FibreC makes this possible— a material that spans the gap between fiber-reinforced plastics and reinforced concrete through an extrusion process that incorporates bundles of glass fiber into thin sections of concrete. An advance over steel-reinforced concretes, this method allows thinner sections to be made that are also lighter, thanks to the lower density of glass (as opposed to steel rebar), and the change from oriented bundles of fibers in the core to a random mesh at the surface, which maximizes the performance of the glass in the panel. Ultimately, this composite-like method allows for thinner, more sculptural shapes than are possible with existing concrete formulations.

When designing the pavilion, Huang and Dempsey, both AADRL graduates, worked with Hanif Kara of AKT II to engineer a balance between the forward-thinking designs of the DRL and an air of social engagement. Although the total structure is small, a sense of openness and exchange prevails through its semi-open form, which facilitates movement through the pavilion and seating area and encourages chance encounters. But the structure's communal spirit is perhaps most viscerally expressed in its construction: all 800 panels of mesh were hand-assembled by students and staff.

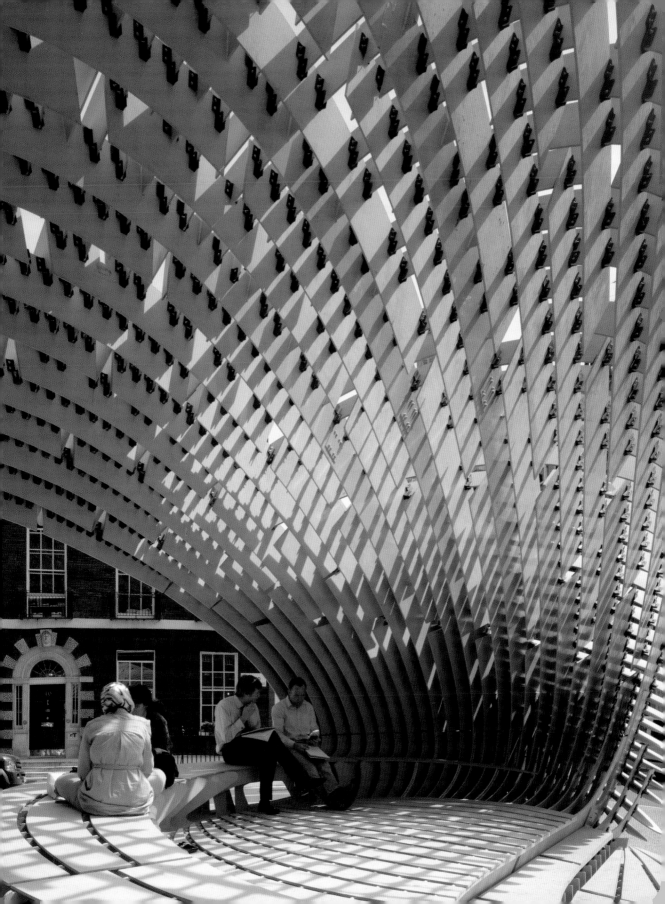

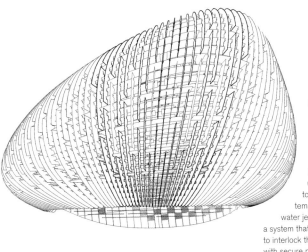

left and right Huang and Dempsey started with thirteen flat 13-mm (0.5-in.) sheets of fibreC. They designed 850 unique profiles and used CAD software to design cutting templates for a CNC water jet. The team created a system that required four steps to interlock the composite profiles with secure neoprene gaskets.

below and opposite The pavilion celebrates the tenth anniversary of the Architectural Association's Design Research Laboratory, which has devoted much to the intersection of material research and computational architecture.

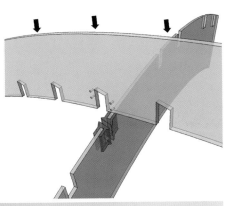

LILLE MÉTROPOLE MUSEUM OF MODERN ART

CLIENT
Lille Métropole Communauté Urbaine

ARCHITECT
Manuelle Gautrand Architecture

MATERIAL ENGINEER
Khephren Ingénierie (structural engineers),
Lafarge (manufacturer)

LOCATION
Villeneuve d'Ascq, France

COMPLETION
2010

SIZE
2,700 m² / 29,063 ft²

MATERIAL
Fibrous ultra-high-performance concrete
(UHPC)

RELATED MATERIALS
MC# 5058-09, MC# 6242-01, MC# 6421-02,
MC# 6479-01

opposite The museum's
extension is constructed of five
root-like structures oriented
along a gentle slope of the
nature reserve known as the
Parc du Héron.

French architect Manuelle Gautrand's ribbon-like addition to the Lille Museum of Modern Art (LAM), originally designed by Roland Simounet in 1983, is a vivid extension of the Flemish-accented city's place on the cultural map. First designed to house early twentieth-century works acquired by French collector Roger Dutilleul, the original brick and glass structure contained galleries plus a library, educational department, and offices. Faithful to the tenets of modernism, Simounet's low-rise assemblage of pavilions, now a historic landmark, anchors the complex with orthogonal rigor.

By contrast, Gautrand's extension is arrestingly fluid with lacy, perforated concrete walls that wrap around the north and east sides of the building as a showcase for the museum's Art Brut collection—often-fragile works created by self-taught or naïve art makers who possess little or no contact with the mainstream art world. The new addition fans out into a series of meandering skeins that unbraid themselves as they extend into the park-like setting. At the farthest end of each gallery, cutouts in the wall create a perforated screen that is deferential to its context, modulating low light levels to protect the works on display while offering views out into the landscape.

To construct the thin shells that contain the galleries required concrete of the highest quality. Taking its cues from the evolution of nanotechnology, Ductal ultra-high-performance concrete takes the basic formulation of concrete and, by controlling the constituents on a nano-scale, is able to enhance the properties of the material to create a substance with compressive strength ten times that of standard concrete. Incorporating super-plasticizers into the mix increases the material's strength and moves it closer to the composite arena, where the inherent toughness of the epoxy resin complements the stiffness but avoids the brittleness of glass or carbon fiber. Steel strengthening fibers are also added to further enhance the strength of the bent cast pieces, enabling a stronger, thinner, finer casting of exterior structural façades while reducing material volumes and pushing concretes into the realm of composites.

left and below left The aerial view shows how the complex roof and the resin finish on the roof help the structure to recede into the landscape, while the plastic model shows how the ribbed structure fans out into galleries at the east end and contracts to shelter a café-restaurant.

below right and opposite The architects designed a "biomorphic motif" for the concrete screens that enabled them to adjust the size of each opening enough to allow 30 percent of the glass bays to remain unobstructed to light. On-site pouring of the walls was done in an almost artisan-like manner with timber formwork to avoid the need to cast molds to adapt to the apertures' constantly changing dimensions.

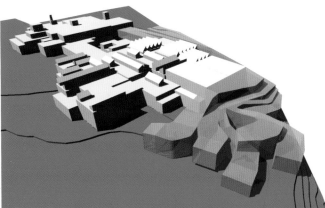

STEDELIJK MUSEUM

CLIENT
City of Amsterdam

ARCHITECT
Benthem Crouwel Architects

MATERIAL ENGINEER
Solico (façade consultant), Holland
Composites (manufacturer)

LOCATION
Amsterdam, The Netherlands

COMPLETION
2012

SIZE
12,000 m² / 129,167 ft²

MATERIAL
Vacuum-injection-molded panels
reinforced with Tejin's Twaron and
Tenax super fiber

RELATED MATERIALS
MC# 1254-03, MC# 4569-01,
MC# 6354-01, MC# 6780-01

opposite top High-performance
fibers from Japan were used to realize
the extension to the museum. The
two exhibition areas are seamlessly
connected by underground escalators.

opposite bottom The composite
roof material is also used in the columns.
Twaron and Tenax fibers were combined
to give designers a lightweight, stable,
and impact-resistant material.

overleaf The white volume is also
known as "the bathtub" because of
the basin-like, seamless appearance
afforded by the roof's reinforced-fiber
construction.

For 800 years, Amsterdam has proved adept at burnishing the old and welcoming the new, making it an ideal setting for shaking up cultural complacencies. During the twentieth century, the flamboyant red-and-white-striped, neo-Renaissance Stedelijk Museum, designed by Adriaan Willem Weissman in 1895, stood out as a highlight of the city's trailblazing design and contemporary art movements.

But with the arrival of the digital age and the consequent evolution of viewer expectations, the Stedelijk's spatial limitations became apparent, coupled with outdated mechanical systems that prevented curators from borrowing art that required a controlled environment. Fueled by a desire to update, expand, and reorient the building to better engage with Museumplein (Museum Square), the Stedelijk embarked on an ambitious expansion plan. The resulting design makes a clean break with Weissman's elaborate architectural language through a pristine, minimalist façade whose oblong shape and rooftop flange prompted the dubious moniker "the bathtub."

With a length of 100 meters (330 feet), the smooth, flat exterior required careful planning and ingenious design, resulting in what is said to be the largest composite building envelope in the world. Among the façade's more remarkable features is the material that permits the creation of the seamless white surface: panels of a new composite material whose key ingredient is a synthetic fiber called Twaron. Usually used for the hulls of motorboats, aerospace and industrial components, and sports equipment, Twaron is used here for the first time as a large-scale architectural surface. It not only provides an exceptionally uniform surface but also permits the construction of a building shell five times as strong as steel with less than half the weight of a normal curtain wall.

With the space-age annex and the original building now joined, the fanciful Dutch gables and pyramidal turrets look crisper and more exuberant than ever. Inside the famous white-walled galleries, visitors enjoy a more focused, better-lit, climate-controlled experience. And a new ground-level plaza that spills out on to Museumplein has further woven the Stedelijk into Amsterdam's public life.

"Particles of Dark Matter" is a series of sculptures by Korean artist Jang Yong Sun, who recycles common iron pipes into cellular forms that exhibit iron's strength in tension. Simyo Gallery / Jang Yong Sun.

CHAPTER 4
DIGITALLY FABRICATED METALS

Though concrete has the dubious accolade of constituting the largest volume of any human-made material on the planet, metals are clearly the winner when it comes to ubiquity, versatility, and sheer influence in the design of our manufactured world. The modern age is defined by our use of metals, with skyscrapers, transport, weapons, and *the machines to make everything else* being predominantly metal. But as we head into the twenty-first century, we see predictions of the fall of the preeminence of this class of materials, and a move toward a biological, grown, more natural future, including nanotech that uses carbon, cellulose, ceramics, biotech, and other non-metallics.

These predictions have arisen mainly because metals, most notably our workhorse, steel, have hit a rut in terms of innovation. Plastics, composites, natural materials, ceramics, have all made significant advances when it comes to property improvements, whereas metals have not moved much in the last twenty years, or at least not far enough for us to consider anything particularly new or groundbreaking. Indeed, there are some who believe metals an outdated class, at their limits of performance, and always so *heavy*, but let us take a step back and consider where our use of metals currently stands and where there may be room for further innovation yet.

RECYCLING

Metals are always reusable. Steel and aluminum are heavily recycled; in fact metals are overall the most effectively reused class of materials. Structural metals such as carbon steel (by far the most used metal in construction), stainless steel (more expensive but does not need painting), and aluminum have global recycling rates of between 60 and 85 percent. These rates could easily reach 100 percent without compromising performance, but owing to the delicate balance of global pricing of these commodity metals, if the amount significantly increases (say to an average of 90 percent), the price becomes unstable, making virgin steel cheaper. Metals also have the advantage of being infinitely recyclable, meaning that the steel used to construct the Burj Khalifa in Dubai probably contains steel from buildings or cars scrapped in the 1950s, then again in the 1970s, and so on. This phenomenon is even more surprising for precious metals such as gold, where a wedding ring made this year may well contain gold mined in South America in the 1500s. This permits us to consider metals in the long term, as materials we will have with us for many generations to come. This gives them a history, but also gives us a responsibility when it comes to their use and reuse.

METAL ALLOYING

The alloying and heat-treating of metals, essential for us to have transitioned from the Iron Age to the Industrial Revolution, enables us to make steel stainless, and gives aluminum its "aerospace" performance (pure aluminum is useless as a performance metal), but significant improvements through more or better alloying of steel

below Joris Laarman designed the Bone Chair (here in aluminum) with optimization software that mimics the ability of trees and bones to grow material where strength is needed and take it away where it is unnecessary, creating the minimum structure necessary to support a given weight.

above Arcam's Electron Beam Melting technology is capable of generating one-off custom implants built with data derived from CT scans of individual patients.

opposite The BCN/Sant Cugat/iGuzzini Illuminazione Ibérica HQ by MiAS Arquitectes in Barcelona was designed with a textile screen stretched over a three-dimensional metallic structure.

or titanium are unlikely to give us substantial improvements over what we have now. It would appear that we have just about fully tapped what metals can do on their own. One notable exception to this is the area of amorphous metals, also known as metallic glasses or glassy metals. These can be found in smaller items such as the cases of high-end phones, golf-club heads, and some high-performance engineering products. They are created by taking an alloy based on titanium or zirconium and cooling it so quickly that it is "frozen" into a liquid-like structure that has an internally random formation. Making titanium and zirconium alloys amorphous gives them incredible hardness and energy rebound. Indeed, certain titanium amorphous alloys are three times the strength of other titanium alloys and approach the elastic modulus of bone (a rare feat). This area continues to be expanded in the smaller consumer product arena, but is currently nonexistent in any architectural materials, mainly because with their greater strength also comes greater likelihood of fracture.

The next generation in the evolution of metals will come only when we can combine them intimately with other materials such as plastics, ceramics, and even natural materials to create a synergistic increase in strength to weight. We have seen this on a basic level using ceramic additives to metals to create "cermets" that are used as drill bits,

replacement hip joints, lightweight armor, and watch casings. However, the mixture of the two materials is still relatively random and coarse, and will need to be much more closely controlled to achieve the improvements we want to see.

MALLEABLE MATERIALS

Despite the current limitations in innovation and the creeping conquest by plastics in many smaller applications, metals continue to dominate several areas of architecture thanks to one noteworthy attribute—ductility within close tolerances. The manageably ductile nature of metals means that they are able to withstand forces and events that would destroy other structural materials. Their ability to flex and bend, expand and contract again and again without losing their strength means there is currently no other material class that architects can depend upon in the same way for their structural needs.

This ductility also enables steels and other metals to be sculpted, shaped, cut, folded, or perforated, while knowing how the material will behave in terms of strength. It is this unique attribute, combined with modern computer-controlled routing, perforating, folding, and shaping apparatus, that has given metals a new lease of life. We now see steels, brass, titanium, aluminum, copper, on the faces of buildings, with dendritic organic forms, meshes that mimic

the effect of light passing through trees, the appearance of flower petals: all possible owing to the intricate forming of these ductile materials and the computer-aided knowledge of how thin, how fine, how hollow, how perforated they can be made. Perforation, for example, becomes functional, reducing weight where not needed; and indeed, because of the propensity of some metals to being work-hardened, often the act of perforation can add stiffness by the force of the cutting-out of the hole. Decorative façades that mimic organic structures, such as Thom Faulder's Airspace Tokyo, show the way in which these types of form could develop.

And with these computer-controlled intricacies, could the next step be the fine detail we see in truly organic forms such as bones, seashells, plant stems, giving metals increased strength to weight simply thanks to the internal and surface structure of the form? Could titanium, if shaped with the exact same internal structure as bird bones, give us lighter, stronger beams that offer longer spans, more airy buildings? This is the next step in the evolution of computer-controlled metal-forming. In the way that Joris Laarman has taken a biomimetic approach to design with the Bone Chair, automotive designers are achieving similar things with space frames of cars. How does this translate to architecture—to enable modular space frames to create buildings, perhaps?

ORANGE CUBE

CLIENT
Rhône Saône Développement

ARCHITECT
Jakob + Macfarlane Architects

MATERIAL ENGINEER
T.E.S.S. (façade consultant)

LOCATION
Lyon, France

COMPLETION
2011

SIZE
6,300 m² / 67,813 ft²

MATERIAL
RMIG customized aluminum mesh

RELATED MATERIALS
MC# 5406-01, MC# 5492-01,
MC# 6309-01

opposite The perforated façade of the Orange Cube was designed to let in a precise amount of light and air, but the pixelated pattern of apertures was aesthetically driven by the flow of the Saône River below.

Even Francophiles are often surprised to learn that Lyon, France's third-largest city, is not only its gastronomic capital but has been a site of great commercial and strategic significance since before the first century. Situated at the confluence of the Rhône and the Saône rivers, Lyon possesses a rich urban fabric and architectural history. Its civic vibrancy is reflected in the decision in 2007 to revive its waterfront by transforming 150 hectares (370 acres) of prime docklands real estate into a commercial and cultural center. Among the anchors for this revitalized sector is a boldly colored structure wrapped in a dramatic perforated skin: the Orange Cube.

Perched on the riverfront, the six-story box is an eye-catching play on color and geometry, solid and void. The building's most striking architectural move is the three conical openings oriented toward the water. Physically, the large piercings allow light and air to penetrate deep into the core of the structure, while symbolically the building opens up to the cityscape and its evolving edge.

Equally compelling is the building envelope, a veil of twenty-five aluminum panels composed of laser-cut and press-punched openings that dance across the surface and mimic the movement of water. The panels are attached to a steel frame that sheaths the building's primary façade, painted a deeper shade of orange, which, visible underneath, provides depth and texture.

Today, there are few limitations to the patterns that can be made by perforating metals such as aluminum for architectural façades. The best way to determine the pattern and degree of openness of the perforation is typically by understanding the amount of light that is needed for the interiors (2 percent for this façade), and the amount of heat transfer desired, as well as, of course, aesthetic preference.

All three aspects succeed in this "thermo-lacquered" aluminum façade that injects the area with new energy. The color, additionally, brings an ironic note, picking up the orange of lead paint typically used in industrial ports.

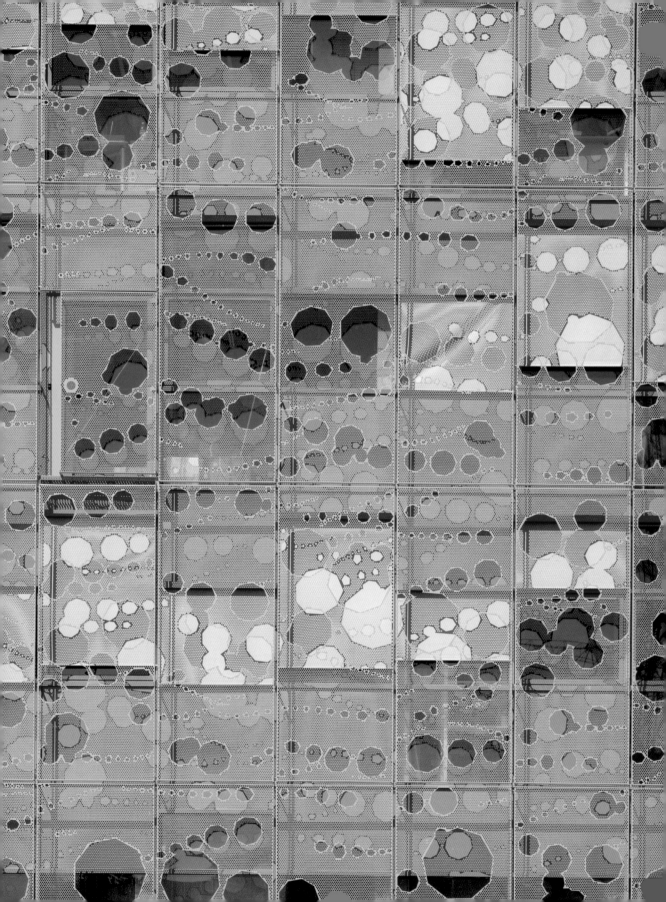

right The architects used structural form and façade engineering to open up the structure and bring cool breezes from off the water into the building.

below By removing a conceptual cone from the Cube Jakob + Macfarlane created a new double-height space, insulated by a faceted thermal façade.

opposite The architects describe the conic voids as "volumetric perturbations" because of the way they interrupt the standard metallic pole-girder structure.

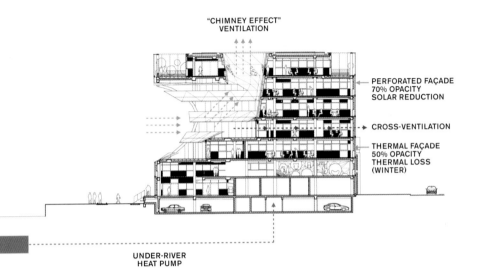

"CHIMNEY EFFECT" VENTILATION

PERFORATED FAÇADE 70% OPACITY SOLAR REDUCTION

CROSS-VENTILATION

THERMAL FAÇADE 50% OPACITY THERMAL LOSS (WINTER)

UNDER-RIVER HEAT PUMP

41 COOPER SQUARE

CLIENT
Cooper Union

ARCHITECT
Morphosis Architects

MATERIAL ENGINEER
Gordon H. Smith Corporation
(façade consultant)

LOCATION
New York City, USA

COMPLETION
2009

SIZE
16,258 m² / 175,000 ft² (gross area)

MATERIAL
Perforated steel mesh panels

RELATED MATERIALS
MC# 1437-06, MC# 5588-02, MC# 5946-06,
MC# 6557-02, MC# 6991-01

opposite The perforated-steel solar façade seems to deform around the interior volume, shifting and opening up for a nine-floor atrium that rises through the building.

overleaf left Morphosis relied on digitally integrated construction methods to realize the atrium. Instead of drawing, architects designed in a 3D environment and worked with contractors to refine details with digital tools before anything materialized.

overleaf right 41 Cooper Square was the first LEED- (Leadership in Energy and Environmental Design) certified academic laboratory building in New York City and its design should be credited as much to the material engineers, contractors, and manufacturers as to the architects.

A t the Cooper Union for the Advancement of Science and Art on Manhattan's Lower East Side, Morphosis Architects, the Santa Monica-based firm of the Pritzker Prize-winning architect Thom Mayne, has given the city a new landmark in the form of a brave, sculptural building that displays a daring use of materials. The architects' response to the need for a new academic building begins with a perforated-metal exterior that is curved in both plan and section. This shimmering surface sheaths a poured-in-place concrete structure whose goal is to foster collaboration and cross-disciplinary exchange among the 150-year-old institution's three schools: art, architecture, and engineering. Custom-punched by Zahner, a Kansas City-based sheet-metal manufacturer that has worked with Morphosis on previous projects, the stainless-steel outer skin provides a 50 percent reduction in solar heat load for the building, just one of several sustainable features that help to conserve energy. But it also determines its overall visual character, a gritty elegance that speaks to the area's creative capital.

Inside, a central atrium rises nine floors, accessible at the lower level by a grand central stair that draws circulation up through the building. The undulating void created by the atrium is wrapped in a glass-fiber-reinforced gypsum lattice, challenging the notion of a college campus as an unfolding sequence of bounded, exterior spaces, and proposing a reevaluation of the modern urban campus.

The tough, torn appearance of the façade that faces Cooper Square at Fourth Avenue also offers a lesson in materials as inspiration. The folded metal skin mimics the tiny imperfections that appear in such alloys as stainless steel when they are bent, deformed, or perforated. Known as "dislocations," these microscopic tears in the lattice-like structure of the steel (very much like the panel structure of the façade) actually boost its stiffness and are an effective way of improving metals. Thus, the large overall metal exterior magnifies the structure of the material that it is made from, so that beauty is aligned with industry, and imperfections become a part of the whole.

ORDOS ART & CITY MUSEUM

CLIENT
Ordos City

ARCHITECT
MAD Architects

MATERIAL ENGINEER
SuP Ingenieure GmbH, Melendez & Dickinson
Architects (façade/cladding consultants)

LOCATION
Inner Mongolia, China

COMPLETION
2011

SIZE
41,227 m² / 443,764 ft²

MATERIAL
Powder-coated erosion-resistant
aluminum panels

RELATED MATERIALS
MC# 0247-02

opposite top The steel single-truss
stiffened-shell structure was built on
a plateau in Kangbashi New Area, an
uninhabited part of Ordos City.

opposite bottom Exposed to winds
from the desert, construction workers
join the standing seams between the
aluminum "ribbons" of building skin that
were delivered preassembled to the
building site.

overleaf Assembled by hand and
designed using steel-specific CAD
software at the China Academy of
Building Research, the museum sets
a striking precedent for architects and
designers in Ordos and beyond.

Seen from above, the city center of Ordos in
northern Mongolia is a crisp urban grid of
impressive scale superimposed on an arid steppe
landscape. Within each quadrant, it is easy
to make out distinct architectural forms and
the orthogonal layout of a city plan that was conceived as
a whole and drawn up from scratch. One form, however,
pushes against this order, its organic shape suggesting a
found object rather than something manmade—the Ordos
Art and City Museum.

Set on a reinforced-concrete slab that refers to the
surrounding Ordos Plateau, the museum suggests a smooth
polished stone that mediates between the earth and the
sky. The futuristic structure is ingeniously composed in
two parts: a steel and reinforced-concrete interior overlaid
with a horizontal ribbon exterior, which was designed using
3D software to achieve a "single layer grid shell structure."
The undulating standing-seam dome is composed of matte
3-millimeter (0.12-inch) thick aluminum panels onto
which an additional powder coating has been applied as
an erosion-resistant surface, protecting against the ravages
of the Gobi Desert. The aluminum sheets themselves offered
a lightweight yet strong material capable of providing
additional support to the overall skin structure. Each
component was prefabricated, then assembled on site.

Despite the grandeur conveyed by its soaring
undulations and enclosed, iconic form, the museum seeks to
tell a local story based on the cultural history of the region.
Inside, gallery spaces are divided between two separate
internal towers that connect via pedestrian bridges, an
arrangement intended to offset such natural forces as wind
and earthquakes. Irregularly shaped swaths of glazing invite
light into expansive, curving galleries, artfully alluding to the
rounded enclosures of traditional Mongolian yurts.

BLOOM

CLIENT
Materials & Applications

ARCHITECT
Doris Sung with DOSU Studio Architecture

MATERIAL ENGINEER
DOSU Studio Architecture

LOCATION
Los Angeles, California, USA

COMPLETION
2012

SIZE
6 m² / 65 ft²

MATERIAL
Thermo-bimetal panels: jointed thin metal plates with slightly different coefficients of expansion

RELATED MATERIALS
MC# 5457-01, MC# 5519-01

opposite top Doris Sung and her firm DOSU Studio Architecture challenged the hegemony of the static building skin by utilizing the natural response of the metallic materials to heat.

opposite bottom Sheet thermo-bimetals are a smart material because they curve in precise ways in response to heat, according to the capacities of their constituent metallic materials.

overleaf Smart materials enabled Sung to conceive of the structure as a plant. Her challenge was to "grow" Bloom on a very narrow site—akin to a crack in the sidewalk—from which a lightweight, robust, beautiful, and performative construction could emerge.

Even before you see the undulating metallic structure inserted between two buildings in the Silver Lake section of Los Angeles, the name—Bloom—conveys its intent. Doris Sung, who conceived of Bloom, teaches architecture at the University of Southern California but looks to biology for inspiration, in particular the dynamic possibilities of "smart" materials. Her environmentally responsive installations offer prototypes for how we might design beautiful, climatically sensitive structures that meet real human needs. "Plants and other things in nature have a performative purpose, *and* they are beautiful," she explains. Constructions such as Bloom "test material behavior, structure, digital fabrication tools, and more. The fact that they look like art or a product of beauty is part of my obligation as an architect to consider all the virtues of design."

Bloom's striking shape is composed of laser-cut bimetallic plates that have been riveted together. The 6-meter (20-foot) tall "shelter" tracks the sun, responding to changes in heat and light. Fourteen thousand individual strips curve and let in greater amounts of air when the structure heats up, then bend back to their original position once the temperature diminishes. The canopy even curls shut when the sun is directly overhead. Rather than being a static, protective shield, the surface is flexible and responsive, instinctively acting like a shutter system and, thereby, reducing the need for artificial cooling.

Bloom underscores the multitude of opportunities that exist for nature and the built environment to work synergistically in ways that we are only beginning to envision.

To achieve its intelligent effect, the structure relies on the different thermal expansions of two metal strips bonded together, with heat causing them to bend. Typical examples of this are copper/steel and brass/steel sheets, the copper expanding more and becoming the outside surface of the curve. The same effect has been used for years in on/off switches for electric kettles, in meat thermometers, and to ensure that clocks run accurately despite changes in temperature.

SOUMAYA MUSEUM

CLIENT
Carlos Slim Foundation

ARCHITECT
FR-EE Fernando Romero Enterprise

MATERIAL ENGINEER
Geometrica (façade system and fabrication)
with Gehry Technologies

LOCATION
Mexico City, Mexico

COMPLETION
2011

SIZE
16,000 m² / 172,223 ft²

MATERIAL
Parametric steel lattice with outer skin
of laser-cut aluminum hexagonal panels

RELATED MATERIALS
MC# 1627-08, MC# 6249-01, MC# 6793-01

opposite The Soumaya
Museum's floated aluminum skin
required highly synchronized
coordination between architects,
3D engineering specialists, and
fabricators, who laser-cut more
than 16,000 panels for the
10,000-m² (107,600-ft²) façade.

The museum world has delivered some audacious structures but few are as eye-popping as the Museo Soumaya in Mexico City. Designed to house the art collection of a single individual, Mexican telecom billionaire Carlos Slim, it is a shimmering showcase for an eclectic range of works. Its 66,000 pieces include works by Leonardo, Toulouse-Lautrec, Picasso, Dalí, Rivera, and Renoir, as well as religious relics and coins. The pristine, largely opaque interiors fend off the urban clamor of the surrounding area but are meant to do more than simply create an atmosphere of quiet contemplation. They are the core of a structure designed to shape public space, part of a large-scale, mixed-use urban redevelopment of a former industrial zone.

The anvil-shaped, six-floor building rises up from a concrete pedestal with voluptuous curves of silvery aluminum hexagonal panels that stretch across the surface like a skin. Such creative form-making is the work of Fernando Romero, the client's son-in-law, whose futuristic design is an ode to Slim's late wife, the museum's namesake.

The building's most compelling feature is its exterior, a multilayered construction composed of a steel skeleton, a triangular frame substrate onto which a base layer of galvanized-steel rhombuses is secured, followed by a two-layer waterproofing membrane, then structure connectors that hold the outer panels at the correct orientation. The structure connectors provide supports for the fittings to which the 16,000 aluminum hexagons can attach at their centers, giving Romero's desired "floating" look to the building envelope. Multiple families of hexagon sizes and shapes were used, creating an exact fit for all the pieces over the convoluted surface, with three different clear powder-coating types used to further protect the aluminum panels from weathering depending on the location of the panel.

above The panels sweeping around the finished building seem to float (right, and opposite top). To achieve this effect, dome-building experts at Geometrica devised a support system of rhomboid decking panels that connects the surface panels to a triangular steel lattice suspended from the core columns (left).

left The surface orientation and curvature of Fernando Romero's model varied at every point, so the 3D specialists at Gehry Technologies scanned the model and mapped "families" of hexagonal panels with similar geometries for fabrication.

opposite The sixth (top) floor holds an important collection of sculptures by French sculptor Auguste Rodin. It offers a view of the engineering masterwork that is the skylight hub, where the twenty-eight columns that hold up the building meet.

"LABRYS FRISAE"

CLIENT
Shimon Bokovza, director of Graffiti Gone
Global, owner of Sushi Samba

ARCHITECT
Marc Fornes / THEVERYMANY

MATERIAL ENGINEER
Marc Fornes / THEVERYMANY

LOCATION
Miami, Florida, USA

COMPLETION
2010

SIZE
9.1 x 5.5 m / 30 x 18 ft

MATERIAL
Digitally fabricated aluminum panels

RELATED MATERIALS
MC# 6833-01

opposite top Architect Marc
Fornes designed this non-linear
installation to resemble three-
dimensional inhabitable graffiti.

opposite bottom Renderings
of "Labrys Frisae" show how the
installation's curling surfaces can be
seen from the mezzanine above and
approached from three access points
on the lobby floor.

overleaf Called "computational
skinning" by Marc Fornes, the installation
contains a total of 10,322 parts. It would
have been impossible to design without
algorithms, and difficult to build in any
other material besides metal.

With its gold-tinged panels that riff on bones, shells, and flower petals, this exuberant pavilion assembled for Art Basel Miami looks grown rather than built, organically coaxed into shape rather than computer-scripted and fabricated based on computational protocols. In conceiving of the design, though, French architect Marc Fornes of THEVERYMANY was less concerned with botany than with exploring how to apply the principle of surface tension to a taut, complex environment made from simple, inexpensive parts. To realize the fluted volumes, thin sheets of powder-coated aluminum were cut into 10,000 separate parts and then stitched together with more than 100,000 rivets, making the skills needed to control the process from design to fabrication to assembly as critical as the detailing of the joints. Indeed, only aluminum sheet offers the stiffness, workability, accurate cutting, and permanence that this unique installation possesses.

The 9.1- x 5.5-meter (30- x 18-foot) pavilion undulates in plan, wrapping around a central supporting column within a rotunda. Three entryways invite the viewer inside, where perceptions shift as they move through and around the work. Die-cut perforations in the solid sheets enhance the material's ability to flex and form while allowing star-shaped patterns of light to filter through openings that are necessary for assembly. The negative spaces created by the complex curves, and the frayed edges, lend an ambiguity that ultimately makes the design less about an object and more about the overall effect of the encounter.

Trained eyes will note references to Ross Lovegrove (technology, materials science, and organic form) and Zaha Hadid (multiple perspective points and fragmented geometry), with whom Fornes trained before going out on his own. His sculptural approach—in this case a common material transformed through software able to link three-dimensional forms with intricate metal-cutting procedures—results in something rich and strange with the surface intensity of a much smaller design constructed by hand.

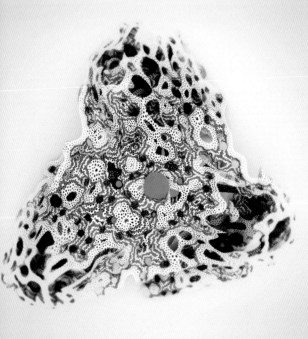

FIDU TECHNOLOGY

CLIENT
ETH, Architonic, Materials Café 2012

ARCHITECT
Zieta Prozessdesign

MATERIAL ENGINEER
Zieta Prozessdesign

LOCATION
Zurich, Switzerland

COMPLETION
2008–12

SIZE
Various

PROCESS
Free Inner Pressure Deformation (FiDU)

RELATED MATERIALS
MC# 5368-01, MC# 5797-01,
MC# 6800-01

opposite FiDU is ideal for traveling exhibitions and installations such as this because the finished stainless-steel components are lightweight, durable, easy to assemble, and striking to experience.

below FiDU is a process using digital and laser production techniques by which two shapes cut out of steel sheets are welded together and inflated.

Structural engineering dictates that a cylinder has a significantly higher strength-to-weight ratio than a flat bar. Thus, laser-cutting thin flat sheets of stainless steel, and welding them along their edges, then inflating them with air until they form a cylindrical balloon that resembles an inflatable toy offers an intriguing way to increase strength.

Over the past decade, Polish-born researcher/designer Oskar Zieta of Zieta Prozessdesign has built on such principals, experimenting with new methods for forming metal, which has led to the development of FiDU Technology (Freie Innen Druck Umformung, or Free Inner Pressure Deformation). By carefully controlling cut shapes and weld lines to avoid creasing, FiDU leverages steel's ability to maintain rigidity in a deformed state as the foundation for a range of evocative, often whimsical designs, many with a pillowy silhouette that gives the cool metallic surface an entirely new dimension. The Plopp family of stools reveal their production process by making kinks and depressions in the inflated steel an integral part of the finished product. The Chippensteel 0.5 chair plays with the past in a handful of glossy, lacquered finishes, while the polished surface of Rondo, a dramatic doughnut-shaped mirror, has a spare elegance.

Equally compelling as it bridges the divide with architecture is the FiDU footbridge, whose astonishing span of 6 meters (20 feet) at a mere 174 kilograms (384 pounds) net weight has helped position FiDU as an innovator in ultralight construction.

For the Architonic Concept Space III at the IMM interior design trade fair in Cologne, Germany, Zieta sought a modular structure that would meet logistical needs (flexible, easy to transport and install) but, more importantly, would make a striking impression, showcasing FiDU as a path toward unexplored applications. Inflated parabolic shapes with arrow-like joints form a pavilion whose basic recurring element is the triangle, a motif that in Zieta's hands feels reductive, futuristic and ready to launch into a multitude of new directions.

above This icosahedron, nicknamed the "FiDU football," was Zieta Prozessdesign's first successful implementation of inner-pressure forming where planned contour control, precision, and the rigidity of ninety separate pieces was involved.

right Rolled-steel profiles created for the London Design Festival were easily shipped from Zurich and inflated on site—here using a bicycle pump.

opposite Blow & Roll FiDU objects not only take up less space in transit, they also—like all FiDU objects—are built additively, without the offcuts that otherwise occur in metal fabrication.

EAST BEACH CAFÉ

CLIENT
Brownfield Catering

ARCHITECT
Heatherwick Studio

MATERIAL ENGINEER
AKT II (structural engineers) with
Littlehampton Welding (fabrication)

LOCATION
Littlehampton, West Sussex, UK

COMPLETION
2007

SIZE
280 m² / 3,014 ft² (built area)

MATERIAL
Prefabricated 8-mm (0.3-in.) thick weathered-
steel sections treated with oil-based coating

RELATED MATERIALS
MC# 5085-01, MC# 6543-01

opposite top The undulating lines
of the weathered-steel exterior are
transposed onto the soft white walls
inside the East Beach Café.

opposite bottom Heatherwick
Studio worked with two local welders
and internationally renowned structural
engineers on the monocoque shell of
the beachside café.

overleaf On a 40-m (131-ft) long
site with a promenade in front and
a sewage line behind, Heatherwick
Studio looked to robust weathered
steel to enchant visitors and protect
them from wind and salt air at the
same time.

L ike a giant mollusk washed up from the sea, the undulating exterior of the East Beach Café proves that potent forms can come from humble structures, in this case a casual seaside eatery. The café's modest scale and gesture of protection from the elements—and from graffiti—gives it an approachable, even intimate, quality that has endeared it to locals and guests. In both the design and the setting it provides a welcome response for an area seeking to revive its popularity.

The metal monocoque exterior—inspired by boat builders—has the earthy hue of rusted steel, a prime example of how metals can age well. Pre-weathering metals is an effective method for changing the appearance of a material type that can all too often be uninspiring in its virgin state, as in the verdigris of the copper roofs of ancient European buildings or the dusty-looking surface of aged zinc. Not all metals take on a patina equally though, and some require assistance to achieve the right look. Pre-weathering for such materials as steel is recommended as the rust layer is so fragile that it falls off, causing more rust to form until the material is completely eaten away. Copper, aluminum, and zinc tend to form a more durable layer that will come off only if scratched, or corroded with acid.

Here, once the rust level was at the desired state, the metal was coated with oil to retard further degradation. The pre-weathering process uses heat and a corrosive environment, sometimes a salt-loaded water bath, to give a more homogeneous surface change rather than the spotty, uneven patina that tends to develop as a result of normal, natural weathering.

Inside the café, a whitewashed room complements the ruddy exterior through a polyurethane foam wall, whose soft forms ripple across the rear. The bank of windows facing the beach seems almost permeable, so that while you are nestled indoors you still feel connected to the outside. No moldings or overtly referential imagery, just wave- and cloud-like contours that echo the sand and shingle to give the impression of a unified whole.

LAVA

INSPIRATION

HONEY COMB STRUCTURE

LIZARD SKIN

BUTTERFLY COCOON

PROJECT

SITE PLAN

UTS TOWER NOW

RE-SKIN UTS

NOCTURNAL SKIN

NIGHT UTS TOWER

INTERIOR SKIN EFFECT

FACADE MATERIALS

A DOUBLE SKIN TO THE BUILDING

TEXTILE PATTERN

SOLAR PANELS INTEGRATED IN THE PATTERN

RELATED PROJECTS

MOET CHANDON MARQUEE, MELBOURNE AUSTRALIA

BEIJING WATERCUBE, with PTW, BEIJING, CHINA

PLASTIC HOUSE, BLUE MOUNTAINS, AUSTRALIA

CHAPTER 5
POLYMER FILMS

Polymer films in architecture offer the tantalizing combination of the transparency of glass with the light weight and structural flexibility of tensile structures. This emerging new material form, though it may still seem somewhat fragile and diaphanous to those used to expecting concrete, steel, and glass in our structures (and it certainly has some current limitations), offers a potential way to reduce weight where it may not be needed, and to free the sometimes rather constricting rigidity of our current structural and glazing solutions.

For this new class of materials, it is the phenomenon of transparency, or at least translucency, combined with flexibility and lightness, that sets them apart from better-known conventional fabric tensile structures, as exemplified by the Millennium Dome in London, the Olympiapark in Munich, and Denver International Airport in the USA. These fabric structures have used glass-fiber textiles coated in PVC or PTFE (Teflon) tensioned across large spans between steel frames to create their distinctive forms. The glass-fiber fabric offers sag-resistant strength in a lightweight material, with the plastic coating covering both sides of this membrane, giving weather resistance, opacity, and the recognizable curved shape.

These tent-like structures that use the tension created by stretching the fabrics across large spans as their defining criteria have always been used as roof structures and are exclusively opaque, trying to mimic the rigid materials they

replace. The new generation of polymer films, however, celebrates its translucent or transparent nature and is beginning to be used also as walls, mimicking glazing and thus taking on glass where glass's transparency has previously always rendered it the only solution.

Polymer films are thin, flexible plastic sheets that have found application as grocery bags, as the transparent layers between architectural glazing, and as the mile-long sheets that protect early-growth agriculture. Most plastics are flexible when you make them sufficiently thin, but not all have the ability to be durable enough and resistant to breaking or tearing with constant use. Even fewer can withstand the demands of outside use, particularly when they need to last for years. Unlike glass, which is a mineral, polymers are organic materials: they are susceptible to aging, light degradation, and oxidation. Translucency and transparency also need to be carefully engineered into the resin and maintained during the various production steps. Only certain plastics can be manufactured with light-transmitting properties, and optical clarity of the type that can rival glass is possible in very few. In addition, sunlight, weathering, and wear and tear reduce clarity, and if you start putting multiple layers or strengthening yarns into the sheet, it takes the "see-through" quality down even further.

Most polymer films are made in pretty much the same way, by melting the plastic resin and then either blowing it up like a long balloon and slitting it open, or extruding

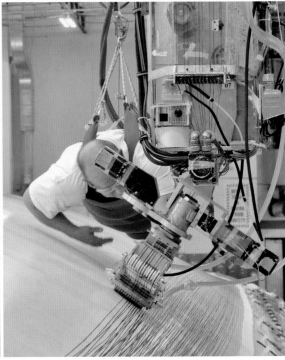

it between successive rollers till it is a few microns thick. Plastic bags, boat wrap, and the clear film used to protect sofas are all forms of this type of film, and are suitable for temporary applications. They are low-cost, widely available, and very easy to manufacture.

But if you need greater durability, higher strength, better resistance to tearing, and the ability to withstand sagging over twenty years—essential in architectural applications—you are likely to need to engineer in greater performance, either by orienting the film, by using multiple layers, or by using engineering polymers.

MANIPULATING THE PLASTIC

Orienting the chains of molecules that make up the polymer film and making them much longer can increase its strength from that of a plastic bag to that of drawn steel. The ropes used to pull tankers are made from roughly the same plastic as Ziploc bags; it is just that the molecules are aligned along the rope's length. Going from the polyethylene (PE) in the Ziploc to ultra-high-molecular-weight polyethylene (UHMWPE) in Dyneema, the commercial name for the yarn used in those ropes, is really a case of joining the molecules together so they are longer, and making them align in one direction. Dyneema is also used in flexible body armor

preceding spread Lightweight, durable polyester stadium wrap from Dow Corning has since been recycled as material for packaging, flooring, and building applications.

above North Sails' 3DL technology uses a laminate of Mylar film and structural yarn precisely applied along predicted load paths for added stability and durability.

opposite A pair of depth-sensing cameras and transparent display made with conductive film allowed Jinha Lee to design the SpaceTop 3D computer with a transparent monitor and 3D gesture control.

and is a common fiber-strengthener in sails for yachts. The immense strength-to-weight ratio of these yarns means that they can be used in super-fine versions, and thus offer support without compromising transparent appearance.

The London 2012 Olympic Stadium wrap is a great example of the wider use of polymers for exterior fabrics, with a polyester lightweight fabric coated in a polyolefin elastomer-based coating. This material allowed the wrap to meet the London Organizing Committee of the Olympic Games's stringent sustainability requirements while ensuring the appropriate fire protection and printability needed for stadium/stage venues.

LAMINATING DIFFERENT FILMS TOGETHER

Laminating numerous thin films together can also give better properties, and this is done routinely for packaging of foods, where one layer is used to protect from sunlight, one for keeping oxygen in (or out), another for keeping carbon dioxide in (or out), one for printing the graphics, and one for strength. This type of multilayering also works for sails that need specific strengths in different locations but little additional weight; and also in the latest computer and mobile phone displays for color, light, power, and protection. KieranTimberlake's much talked about "Smart House" imagined this on an architectural scale, creating a potentially habitable structure that used polyester film as the walls, and layering this plastic with the other functions necessary for standard curtain walls. Roll-to-roll printing of conductive lines was used for the "wiring," with aerogel, ultra-high-insulating glass foam, laid down for temperature control. Metallized films could be used for protection from direct sunlight as they are in modern glazing, with the use of printed digital screens as a way of providing information within the structure. All the technology is currently available, but it has yet to be fully realized on this scale.

ENGINEERING POLYMERS

Since most of the polymer films we encounter in our daily lives are simpler, cheaper commodity plastics such as polyester, PVC, and polyethylene, one way to improve performance is to use more expensive, "engineered" polymers. A good example of this has been the development of fluoropolymers (containing fluorine) such as ETFE, which is in the same family of plastics as PTFE, or Teflon, also used as a membrane in Gore-Tex. ETFE is a transparent high-performance polymer film used as an alternative to glazing in architecture, and has been successfully implemented in high-profile projects such as the Eden Project in the UK and the Water Cube for the 2008 Beijing Olympics. Compared to glass, ETFE film is 1 percent the weight, transmits more light, and costs 24–70 percent less to install, and is thus a viable alternative to much glazing. It does, however, suffer from lower impact strength so has been predominantly used out of the reach of users, such as in skylights or roofing.

THE FUTURE

It is in the combination of these developments that we can expect to see real innovation in polymer films in the architectural space. Greater cut- and impact-resistance can be achieved by the use of strengthening lines of polymer yarns. Dyneema, the oriented long-chain polyethylene yarn used in marine ropes, and Vectran, the yarn used in Nike's Flywire shoes and also a regular solution for yacht sails,

offer high strength with little weight or volume. Newer classes of high-strength plastics known as self-reinforced plastics (SRPs) use different forms of the same plastic to offer strength and flexibility. Self-reinforced polypropylene (SRPP) is used in lightweight suitcases such as the Samsonite Cosmolite and the Tumi Tegralite; the plastic is 100 percent polypropylene, but two different formulations are used— yarns woven into fabrics for the stiffness, and a less stiff, more elastic binding agent to give suitable toughness.

Such developments when applied to other plastics could offer a chance for transparent films that contain strengthening yarns of the same material, giving better impact resistance than currently possible with ETFE. Moving beyond lightweight transparency, the films can be incorporated with high-efficiency insulation using translucent materials such as aerogel laminated onto the surface. In addition, printing of conductive lines provides the equivalent of electrical wires, which can be used to transfer power to outlets or as switches for climate, lighting, and security. Sun protection can be achieved by laminated metallic and nanoceramic films, as exemplified by Huper Optik, or in the use of electrochromic films to provide protection and even privacy when needed, as few would desire a continually transparent living space.

We have begun to see in the last five to ten years a new approach to the use of thin, lightweight polymers as films in architecture. Their traditional drawbacks are being overcome with new formulations, innovative multilayering, and the latest advances in printing to impart additional functionality. Though they may never be suitable for all architectural applications, we can expect to see them broaden the way we see built structures through their light weight, versatility of form, and easy formability.

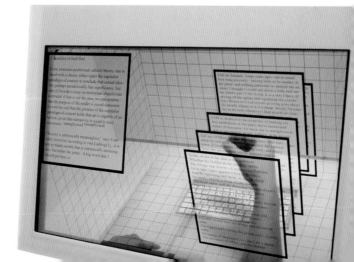

ALLIANZ ARENA

CLIENT
Allianz Arena München Stadion GmbH

ARCHITECT
Herzog & de Meuron

MATERIAL ENGINEER
R+R Fuchs Ingenieurbüro
für Fassadentechnik GmbH
(structural engineers)

LOCATION
Munich, Germany

COMPLETION
2005

SIZE
171,000 m² / 1,840,629 ft²
(total usable area)

MATERIAL
Pressurized-cushion structure of
0.2-mm (0.008-in.) thick ethylene
tetrafluoroethylene (ETFE) foil

RELATED MATERIALS
MC# 5805-05, MC# 6561-01,
MC# 6727-01

opposite Translucent ETFE
cushions fitted with 25,344
fluorescent tubes solved the
formal challenge of designing
a stadium for not one but two
professional football clubs
in Munich.

overleaf left Retractable
fiberglass solar screens were
a complex but necessary
solution (top), while the
translucent ETFE cushions
of the façade were easy
to apply to the stadium's
form (bottom).

overleaf right The
architects specified
polycarbonate panels, but
engineers recommended
ETFE cushions, which
could be made larger to
better fit the architectural
scale of the structure and
would not burn without a
supporting heat source.

Few architects working today have quite the same "touch" that Swiss architects Jacques Herzog and Pierre de Meuron possess. The Pritzker Prize-winning team's portfolio reveals their mastery at transforming a building's skin into a metaphorical canvas upon which function and aesthetics are interwoven in striking ways. From the Ricola cough lozenge factory whose translucent walls are printed with oversized leaves of herbal plants, through the Signal Box auf dem Wolf, whose shimmery copper cladding is twisted at points to admit daylight, to the de Young Museum's perforated and textured façade, the firm has proved remarkably adept at responding to materials and surfaces with innovative treatments and techniques. The Allianz Arena in Munich further reveals its ability to give a structure focused on performance and celebration a dose of sensual engagement with light and materials.

From afar, the stadium's skin resembles glass. In fact, it is sheathed in plastic cushions made of paper-thin ethylene tetrafluoroethylene (ETFE) foil that is inflated by a continuous stream of air. No two of the 2,874 diamond-shaped cushions are alike—a feat of mass customization through computer modeling that gives the stadium a cloud-like appearance. On game nights, 25,344 fluorescent tubes, whose color changes depending on which of the two local football clubs is playing, illuminate the cushions. The stadium glows red for Bayern München, blue for TSV 1860—or white for Germany's national squad.

The most dramatic comparison between transparent ETFE and the glass it resembles is its weight—only 1 percent of the weight of glazing overall, with the thickness of the polymer films a mere 0.2 millimeters (0.008 inches). The exterior hangs like a curtain from a hoop that runs around the structure, with the roof floating on top. The balloon-like form of the double-wall construction provides thermal insulation, warm air being constantly pumped into the pillows to ensure the right shape, with each of the balloons being unique to its frame. To date, cleaning the outside surface of the films has not been necessary since ETFE has a very low surface energy (though not quite as non-stick as its cousin, PTFE, or Teflon) so water rolls right off it, taking the dirt with it.

OLYMPIC SHOOTING VENUE

CLIENT
Olympic Delivery Authority

ARCHITECT
Magma Architecture

MATERIAL ENGINEER
Base Structures Ltd (fabric
structure)

LOCATION
Woolwich, London, UK

COMPLETION
2010

SIZE
14,000 m² / 150,695 ft²
(plot area)

MATERIAL
18,000 m² / 193,750 ft² phthalate-
free polyvinyl chloride (PVC)
membrane

RELATED MATERIALS
MC# 5933-01

It is fitting that an indoor rifle range should resemble a giant target, and the three sleek white structures of the 2012 London Olympics Shooting Venue, punctured by giant red, turquoise, and pink openings, dramatically evoke targets: bold, articulate and, in their resemblance to enormous bits of confetti, celebratory. If you have ever tried to imagine the flow and precision inherent in a sporting process that is largely invisible to the eye, then these buildings act to echo precisely that— supersized. Yet the dots are more than decorative: they identify each building and serve as ventilation, access ways, and tension rings to keep the temporary walls taut.

The three halls form an ensemble outside of the Olympic Park, and for all their iconic presence in the landscape they are intended to be mobile and reusable, so streamlining the form, and thereby the assembly, is integral to the design. The double-curved PVC-membrane façade is stretched, like a swim cap, over a steel armature. Inside, the walls of the shooting area, including deflection panels to protect from ricochets, are clad in plywood. The Olympic Delivery Authority, the client, established tough sustainability criteria, so reduction is the latent theme of these structures: minimal materials, minimal energy consumption, and minimal effort to transport and store.

To make the translucent fabrics used for tension architecture flexible, the PVC used to coat these textiles usually contains phthalates—chemicals that are harmful to hormones in the bodies of humans and animals. The stringent environmental

this page On the historic grounds of the Royal Artillery Barracks in Woolwich, London, the Finals Range is one of three structures designed by Magma Architecture.

above Vibrant tensioning nodes positioned dynamically along the façades were reinforced by modular steel components common in the temporary building industry.

below Built without any composite materials or adhesives for maximum recyclability, the Shooting Venue employs double-curvature geometry to stretch PVC over the maximum area for optimal use.

opposite Steel piles were made out of recycled oil pipes. After use, the structure was fully disassembled and shipped to its next destination, leaving the ground beneath trampled but unbroken.

standards of the London Organizing Committee of the Olympic Games meant that a replacement had to be used that did not contain these toxic additives. Serge Ferrari, one of the leading global suppliers of architectural membranes, developed a membrane that used a phthalate-free alternative, Précontraint 1002 S2 NPP (non-phthalate plasticizer), which still maintained the performance and aesthetics required for this high-profile venue. In addition, through the fabric manufacturer's Texyloop process, all of the fabrics can be effectively recycled for secondary use after the temporary structures are taken down.

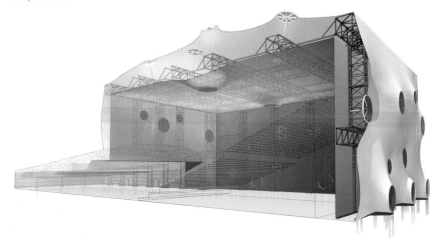

MEDIA-ICT

CLIENT
Consortium of the Zona Franca CZFB
and 22@ of Barcelona

ARCHITECT
Cloud 9

MATERIAL ENGINEER
Agustí Obiol, BOMA (structural engineers)

LOCATION
Barcelona, Spain

COMPLETION
2007

SIZE
3,572 m² / 38,449 ft² (plot area)

MATERIAL
Ethylene tetrafluoroethylene (ETFE)
solar shielding panels

RELATED MATERIALS
MC# 5210-06, MC# 6779-01

opposite The ETFE cushions
have a diaphragm construction,
with three layers and two
air chambers. The first (top)
layer is transparent, while the
second and third are printed
with inverse patterns in metallic
ink. When one chamber is
emptied the patterns line up so
that the cushions are opaque.

A cube composed of four different façades—the most notable a silvery-blue mosaic of convex and concave pillows—the Media-ICT building in the revitalized 22@ district of Barcelona is a true urban catalyst. The goal of 22@ is to drive economic innovation through architectural design that fosters collaboration between technologically advanced companies, research centers, and universities. Media-ICT provides an eight-floor home for the area's ICT (information and communication technologies) community, and a public gathering space for the display and acquisition of digital-age skills. Perhaps more significantly, though, it offers a culturally epochal design that represents a new business model of near-perfect sustainable performance, in which a photovoltaic roof, ETFE skin, and rainwater recycling reduce carbon emissions by 95 percent.

The building's two south-facing façades have been designed to maximize efficiency by harnessing its orientation to the sun. The southeast wall is covered in 106 membranes, or pillows, of ETFE, which slowly inflate and deflate in response to the climate. Each "pillow" is controlled separately, with individual sensors measuring heat, temperature, and the angle of the sun. The ETFE panels go a step further by offering two different solutions to the need for solar energy control. The triangular panels have been printed with metallic ink that acts as a highly effective solar reflector. The pattern of the ink is used to closely control the amount of solar energy and light that enter the building during the projected six hours of direct sunlight daily. In addition, the three-layer construction of the triangular polymer pillows creates up to three static air chambers that increase the façade's thermal insulation.

The long vertical "lenticular" ETFE panel construction on the southwest façade has been designed to act as a light-filtering "cloud" wall. These pillows are filled with nitrogen, a dense gas that blocks more sunlight than air is able to, in much the same way that clouds do.

A similar ingenuity has been brought to the building's engagement with the neighborhood at night. The metal components have been coated with luminescent paint, which charges up during the day and then emits a soft glow once the sun goes down.

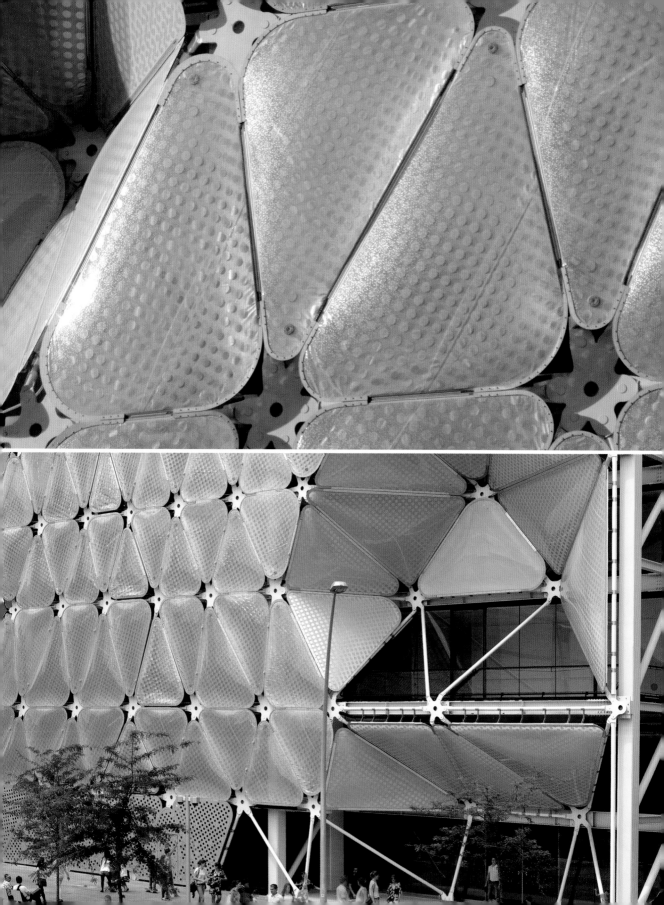

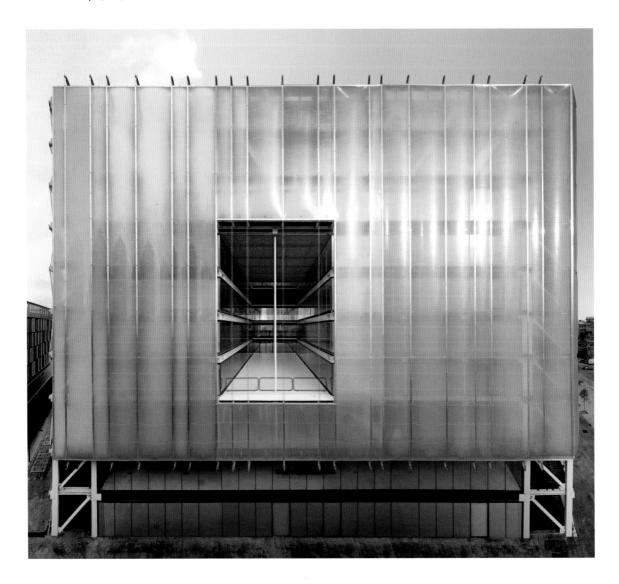

above For the southwest façade, where solar radiation is most intense, structural engineers devised a "lenticular" two-layer construction of transparent ETFE filled with nitrogen to create a cloud-like solar filter.

opposite top In the Media-ICT—and in the age of digitally articulated design— thermal regulation systems move beyond conditioning air indoors to include the precise management of air in the façade itself.

opposite bottom Lead engineer Agustí Obiol designed the steel-truss structure to align this flagship of the digital age with its industrial surroundings.

COCA-COLA BEATBOX PAVILION

CLIENT
Coca-Cola

ARCHITECT
Pernilla & Asif (Pernilla Ohrstedt and Asif Kahn)

MATERIAL ENGINEER
iart interactive ag with AKT II

LOCATION
London, UK

COMPLETION
2012

SIZE
450 m² / 4,844 ft²

MATERIAL
Ethylene tetrafluoroethylene (ETFE) panels sensitive to touch and sound

RELATED MATERIALS
MC# 5019-02, MC# 5210-05, MC# 6550-02

opposite Asif & Pernilla's pavilion takes the potent symbol of the garland into the digital age and up to architectural scale with an inhabitable and interactive ETFE structure.

overleaf, clockwise from top left Interactive media specialists at iart designed cushions that visitors could interact with to trigger sounds of athletes' heartbeats, whistling arrows, sneaker squeaks, and more.

Structural Engineers at AKT II designed a reciprocal frame system of three interacting cushions braced against each other to achieve the pavilion's stable form.

The forty interactive and 190 light-emitting ETFE cushions endured an average of 7,000 visitors per day during the Games.

The conductive silver coating on the inside of the membrane extended the reach of the central sensor that allowed sound designers to manipulate the effects of visitors' distance, velocity, and touch as they moved through the pavilion.

With its radiant color and dynamic composition, this London 2012 Olympic pavilion designed by Pernilla & Asif for Coca-Cola belongs to one of Britain's major traditions of creative expression: music by and for the country's vibrant youth culture. The Beatbox pavilion taps into the relationship between mainstream culture and the legacy of the influence of the nation's underground music (Beatlemania, punk, Britpop, rave) on other creative disciplines, including art and design.

The pavilion's lively exterior is composed of 230 inflated red and white translucent ETFE cushions encased in aluminum frames. An advanced musical interface embedded within the ETFE membranes allows visitors, through gestures and proximity, to tonally engage with the pavilion, triggering and remixing rhythms and sounds associated with Olympic sports. This nest-like arrangement of cushions surrounds a circular steel-frame drum. A spiral aluminum-clad ramp travels around and up the outside of the drum, leading to the pavilion's rooftop and a panoramic view across the Olympic Park. Once there, visitors can enter the pavilion's interior via a black-stained timber ramp that leads to a performance space and, inevitably, a Coca-Cola bar.

The configuration of lightweight ETFE panels required the construction of a reciprocal frame system, with each cushion bracing two others in order to hold the "garland" in place. Although the overall impression is of a random pattern, the pillows on their own are unstable and it is only when a unit of three connects with the others that each achieves the minimum connections required for stability, resulting in a structure whose diverse compositional elements help to transform it from a sound-generating device into a work of architectural ingenuity. Ultimately, it can all be pulled apart and recycled as part of Coca-Cola's 0 percent landfill policy.

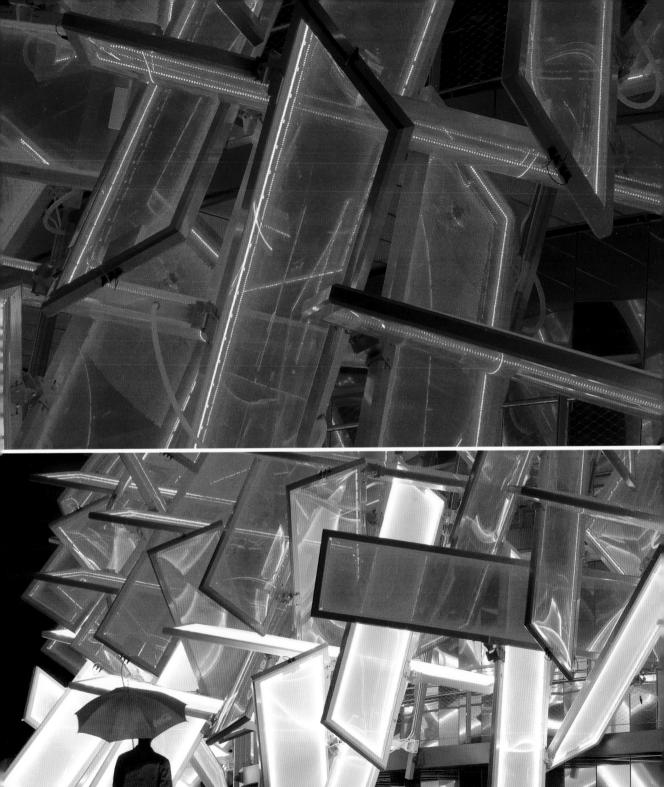

KHAN SHATYR ENTERTAINMENT CENTRE

CLIENT
Sembol Construction

ARCHITECT
Foster + Partners

MATERIAL ENGINEER
Vector-Foiltec (façade consultant, manufacturer)

LOCATION
Astana, Kazakhstan

COMPLETION
2010

SIZE
123,000 m² / 1,323,960 ft²
(total area)

MATERIAL
Ethylene tetrafluoroethylene (ETFE)
tension structure

RELATED MATERIALS
MC# 3487-01, MC# 5963-01,
MC# 6598-01

opposite The joints between the flexible ETFE panels allow the enormous structure to move gently like an accordion, which it does in the extreme climate of Astana.

K han Shatyr is a vast recreation, retail, and entertainment complex in the new Kazakhstan capital of Astana. Yet it is not merely a local diversion from the region's extreme temperatures: it is a portrait of a nation at a turning point in its history. Through the lens of architecture, in this case the world's largest tent, the civic aspirations of a country still new to independence are expressed via a structure whose form acknowledges its precedents—traditional yurts, still a highly efficient way of enclosing a large space.

The nearly 150-meter (500-foot) high tent slopes gracefully up from the northern steppe as if it were part of the landscape. Its most impressive feature is its technically sophisticated roof, a tensile structure held up by a single, central mast that supports a stainless-steel cable system. This, in turn, supports a remarkably transparent exterior made from ETFE cushions, which insulate better and transmit far more natural light than comparable materials. The ETFE cushions are constructed of three layers of transparent polymer film, making the covering lightweight and highly efficient to install. Using steel and glass to cover the same 19,000-square-meter (204,515-square-foot) area that the ETFE covers would have resulted in a very heavy structure, requiring a much more substantial support system and a more rigid form.

The lightweight polymer films not only enable the entire structure to be hung from a central tripod but also allow it to sway with the considerable wind and snow loads during the winter months. "Fritting" (printing of metallic ink patterns) on the outer foil of the cushions creates solar shading, while warm air is pumped up along the interior tent surfaces of the pillow structures to prevent the formation of ice on the inside surfaces of the cushions.

The lightness of the canopy and the transparency of the cushions help to achieve equilibrium between a much-needed gathering place, a green protected zone, and the site's natural geography, forming a physical and symbolic oasis that offers a beacon for the future.

above From the foot of the 20-m (65-ft) tall concrete base one can see the massive three-legged mast that holds a hub structure with a ring 20 m (65 ft) in diameter for the support cables.

opposite Diaphanous in the morning light, the fabric structure expands along extruded aluminum seams as construction workers brave the cold. The fabric roof gently shifts under their feet with the movement of warm air inside.

AIA PAVILION

CLIENT
American Institute of Architects (AIA), New Orleans

ARCHITECT
Gernot Riether with the DFL (Digital Fabrication Laboratory), Georgia Tech

MATERIAL ENGINEER
Russell Gentry, Andres Cavieres

LOCATION
New Orleans, Louisiana, USA

COMPLETION
2011

SIZE
19 m² / 200 ft²

MATERIAL
Glycol-modified polyethylene terephthalate (PETG) cells

RELATED MATERIALS
MC# 4811-01

opposite 352 unique panels form a generative cell structure where each panel is oriented to a particular purpose. Here we can see panels with "wormholes," which save material and help to support the structure.

I ntriguing and futuristic, the AIA New Orleans annual "DesCours" nighttime walking tour (now sadly defunct) was designed to lead visitors through hidden parts of the city by using experimental architecture as a lure. In 2011 German architect Gernot Riether, a professor at Georgia Institute of Technology, proposed a series of glowing spherical enclosures that would be tucked into secret courtyards in the city's sensual, pastel-colored French Quarter, a National Historic Landmark that offered a natural complement to his webbed domes.

Riether's creative focus concerns how digital design and fabrication can lead to new construction methods for environmentally friendly materials. Complex geometry derived from computer modeling has been a hallmark of architecture during the twenty-first century and Riether's pavilion explores these possibilities through the use of a single material: plastic. His lightweight dome uses plastic to construct an affordable, green pavilion whose seemingly random geometry involves 320 carefully composed variations on a single cell, each playing its customized part in a hybrid skin/structure system. When all the cells are assembled, surface tension holds the frame together.

Specifically, the pavilion is constructed with glycol-modified polyethylene terephthalate (PETG) cells, which can be produced from either recycled plastic or sugar cane—a plant that has been integral to Louisiana culture for more than 200 years. This choice of polyester, rather than a fluoropolymer, heralds a new direction in the use of transparent plastics in architecture. PETG has typically been used for interior panels thanks to its clarity and malleability, and, more recently, because it has a lower carbon footprint and toxicity than such alternatives as acrylic and polycarbonate. Indeed, by using sugar cane as the base for the glycol in the resin, purportedly 1 kilo (2.2 pounds) of CO_2 was removed from the atmosphere—by the growing of sugar cane—for every 0.5 kilos (1.1 pounds) of plastic produced. Polyesters still do not have the same overall durability as fluoropolymers, but recent advances in this area of plastics have increased strength and UV resistance, and, of course, lowered their carbon footprint.

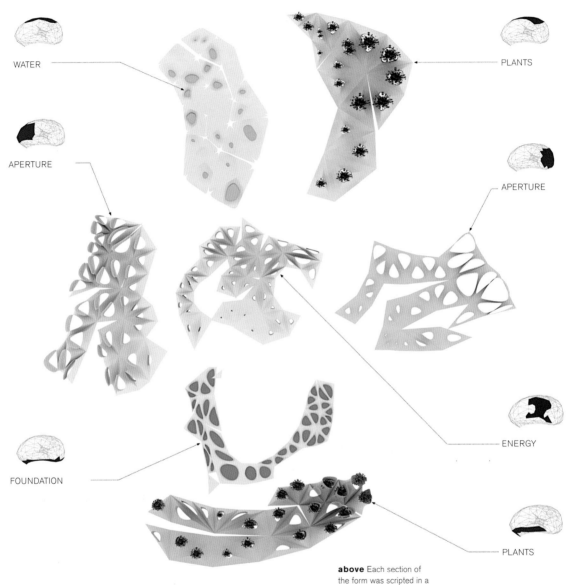

WATER

PLANTS

APERTURE

APERTURE

FOUNDATION

ENERGY

PLANTS

above Each section of the form was scripted in a digital environment to have variable densities given orientations programmed by the architects.

opposite Weighing only 120 kg (265 lbs) in total, the panels of the pavilion were CNC milled from templates and thermoformed. The edges of each piece were folded differently depending on the panel's location within the larger structure.

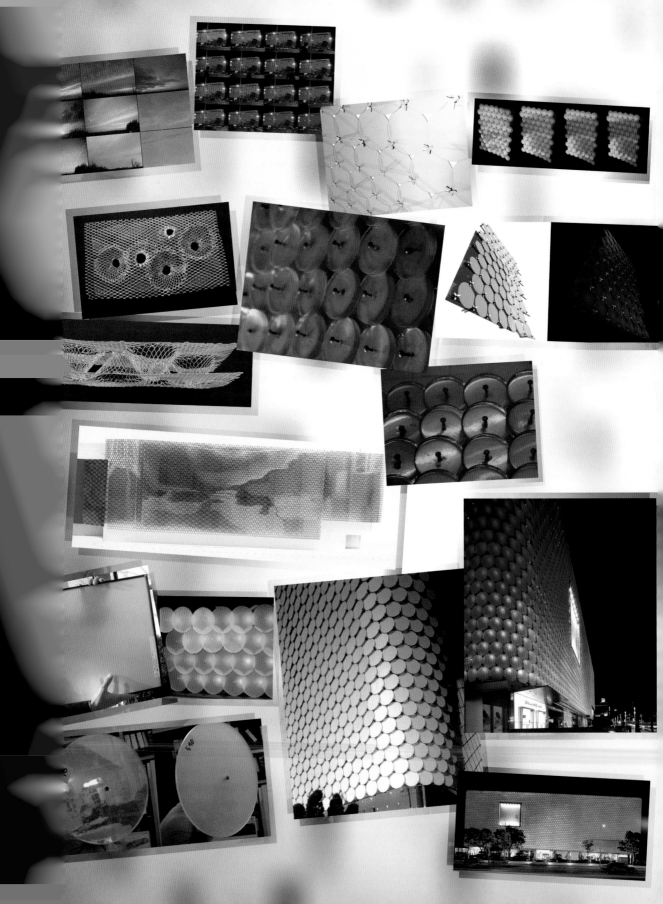

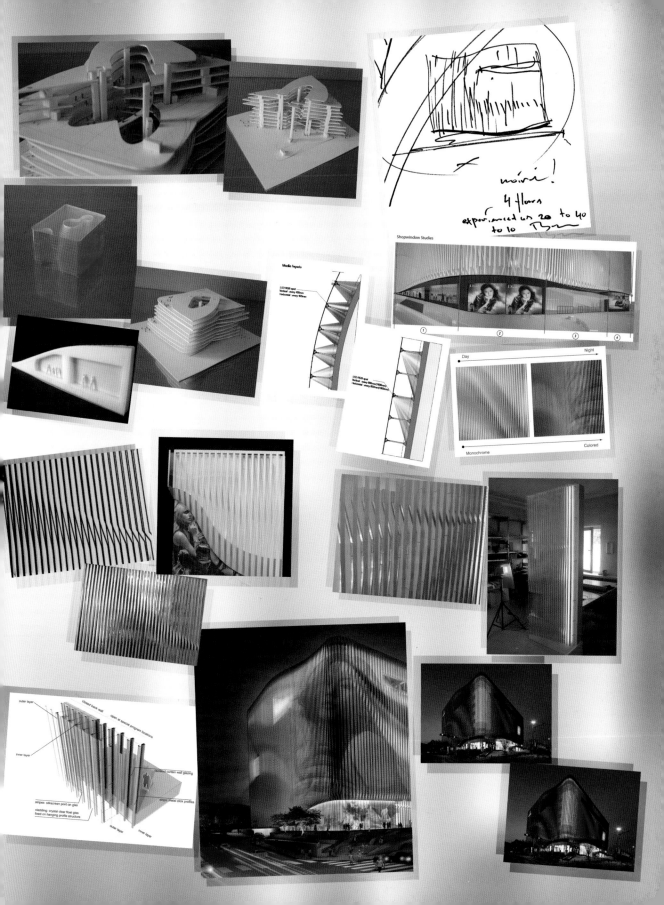

Shopwindow Studies

Media Impacts

Day   Night

Monochrome   Colored

moiré!
4 floors
experienced up 20 to 40
to 10

MATERIALS
DIRECTORY

Material ConneXion is the world's largest library of advanced innovative materials. Our online database gives users access to images, technical descriptions, and usage characteristics, as well as to manufacturer and distributor contact information, all of which has been written and compiled by our international team of material specialists. The content is intended to meet the needs of engineers and scientists as well as architects and designers by providing advanced material expertise in an accessible, user-friendly format. Each material in the database is catalogued with a six-digit MC number: the first four digits identify the manufacturer and the last two indicate how many unique materials are included in the library. Each entry has been juried by a panel of material specialists, architects, designers, and technicians from diverse manufacturing backgrounds. The jury determines whether or not a material warrants inclusion in the library by assessing its inherent innovative qualities. Material innovation is not limited to new materials and technologies. It also includes significant improvements in performance that pave the way for future development, and materials previously used in specialized fields that become more accessible to designers. Innovation also applies to sustainable materials that perform as well as commonly used products but that have a greatly reduced impact on the environment. To learn more, visit: www.materialconnexion.com/books.

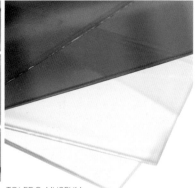

TOLEDO MUSEUM OF
ART GLASS PAVILION
Kazuyo Sejima & Ryue Nishizawa / SANAA
MC# 5554-02
S-LEC™ Acoustic Film
SEKISUI S-LEC™ B.V.
www.s-lec.nl

This flexible, strong, three-ply PVB interlayer material
has been engineered to reduce wind noise and
high-frequency sound for quieter vehicle and building
interiors. The films are available in clear and in "milky
white." Typically, its construction comprises two outer
normal PVB films and an inner acoustic PVB layer. It
is as strong as standard PVB and has improved sound
insulation, particularly in the 1000–5000 Hz range.
Applications are currently for architectural glazing,
dividing screens, and automotive windshields.

TOLEDO MUSEUM OF
ART GLASS PAVILION
Kazuyo Sejima & Ryue Nishizawa / SANAA
MC# 5613-01
LED Embedded Film
SUN-TEC Swiss United Technologies GmbH
www.sun-tec.ch

Advances in digital screens for electronics have led
to conductive clear plastic sheets usable in glazing
that can link up and power LEDs. White or colored
LEDs are embedded onto PVB and connected using a
clear ITO (indium tin oxide) film, offering a waterproof,
durable lighting solution. The LEDs do not emit heat
and may be embedded in a regular array or any
custom pattern required by the client, which can be
controlled in a sequenced light display.

TOLEDO MUSEUM
OF ART GLASS PAVILION
Kazuyo Sejima & Ryue Nishizawa / SANAA
MC# 6851-01
Colored Glass
Glaspro™
www.glas-pro.com

Color in glazing is much simpler if achieved through
the pigmentation of the clear PVB layer which is
sandwiched between the two layers of float glass in
safety glazing. Color matching of this layer is possible
through the combination of multiple layers of film.
The PVB is durable and unaffected by sunlight and
reduces sound vibration.

MUSEUM FOLKWANG
David Chipperfield Architects
MC# 2721-06
Stilla
Joel Berman Glass Studios
www.jbermanglass.com

Using a low-iron composition for this glass removes
the green tinge prevalent in most glazing, essential
in this project where the surface is all curves. The
curves cause more internal reflection, thus a greater
amount of color in the glass. The panes are annealed
to remove stresses before being cast into custom-
designed ceramic molds and then tempered to
increase strength.

MUSEUM FOLKWANG
David Chipperfield Architects
MC# 5163-03
Zerodur®
Schott
www.us.schott.com

This lithium aluminosilicate glass ceramic has much the
same properties as float glass, but has zero thermal
expansion, so it can be used anywhere there are drastic
changes in temperature. It has chemical characteristics
and hardness similar to optical glass and can be
processed using the same machines and tools as optical
and technical glass. Because of this thermal property, it
has been employed to create telescope mirrors, which
retain acceptable figures even in the extremely cold
environments of deep space. It is also used in various
optic applications and precise scientific measurements.

VAKKO FASHION &
POWER MEDIA CENTER
REX
MC# 6148-01
Diamondguard®
Guardian Industries Corp
www.guardian.com

Though glass is durable, it can scratch and soil,
which reduces strength and light diffusion. These
permanent protective coatings provide glass with over
ten times the scratch resistance of tempered and
chemically strengthened glass, thanks to a patented
process of diamond-like carbon deposition on glass.
The panes are low maintenance, guard optical clarity
of the underlying glazing, and are chemically inert.
Applications include transportation, store fixtures and
display cases, and custom tabletops.

VAKKO FASHION & POWER MEDIA CENTER
REX
MC# 6663-01

Glass

Lhotský s.r.o.
www.lhotsky.com

Using an ancient technique of mold-melted glass, these glass tiles are melted together and then slowly annealed in a mold for up to a few weeks. They are then polished to a smooth shine, or sandblasted for a matte finish. The glass varies from transparent to translucent where variable colors are present. They are suitable for use indoors and outdoors with a hard surface. Applications include countertops, tables, interior design elements, wall reliefs, and art objects.

VAKKO FASHION & POWER MEDIA CENTER
REX
MC# 6910-01

Policam Solid Panels
Isik Plastik
www.isikplastik.com.tr

Polycarbonate is finding application in many glazing areas traditionally only possible with glass, with advances in the chemistry of this plastic making it more durable and weather resistant. These solid sheets offer higher impact resistance and lighter weight (half that of glass) than glazing in similar applications. The panels are also easily heat formable, processable, and printable, and can be made more scratch resistant using coatings.

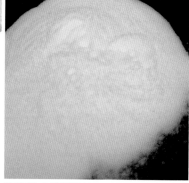

TURNER CONTEMPORARY GALLERY
David Chipperfield Architects
MC# 5350-01

3M™ Glass Bubbles
3M Specialty Materials Division
www.3m.com/microspheres

Hollow glass spheres are crush-resistant, lightweight inert fillers for plastics, insulation panels for construction, and buoyancy aids for undersea vessels. They are added to give lightweight, increased filler loading, with reduced cost, VOC (volatile organic compound) reduction, chemical stability and inertness, and temperature resistance with high strength and low density. They can also be added to paints to improve thermal insulation, chemical inertness, and resistance. Non-combustibility makes them suitable for all architectural areas.

TURNER CONTEMPORARY GALLERY
David Chipperfield Architects
MC# 5538-01

Poraver®
Dennert Poraver GmbH
www.poraver.com

These expanded glass granules are used in construction and as fillers for adhesives and mortar. Produced from recycled waste from the glass-manufacturing industry, the chips are ground into powder then made into spherical pellets using water, a binder and expanding agents and heating to 900°C (1352°F). The pellets are light but have good compressive strength, are heat- and chemical-resistant, and have excellent acoustic and thermal insulating properties. When used with plaster in building applications, they enable greater layer strength with minimal cracking.

ALTERSWOHNEN DOMAT/EMS
Dietrich Schwarz Architekten AG
MC# 4756-01

PCM Granulate: GR-40/42
Rubitherm Technologies GmbH
www.rubitherm.com

Phase-change materials (PCMs) are paraffin-wax-based latent-heat storage materials that undergo a phase change (from solid to liquid or vice versa) at a specified temperature to store or release heat. Thus, these particles can be added as insulation in construction and reduce the overall energy required to heat and cool a building. Granulates are non-toxic and chemically inert with respect to most materials. Applications include underfloor heating, food transport, and latent-heat storage units.

ALTERSWOHNEN DOMAT/EMS
Dietrich Schwarz Architekten AG
MC# 4756-04

Rubitherm® GR
Rubitherm Technologies GmbH
www.rubitherm.com

This porous, glass mineral-based, latent-heat storage material mixed with paraffin produces a granulate that is able to store and release heat energy as it passes through a specified, customizable temperature. Paraffin PCMs are bound to a porous mineral with 35% higher heat storage capacity than typical paraffin, giving an effective means for hot and cold storage. During the solid-to-liquid phase change, the material stays in a non-toxic, solid granular form that is chemically inert with respect to most materials. Applications include underfloor heating, food transport, and latent-heat storage units.

ALTERSWOHNEN DOMAT/EMS
Dietrich Schwarz Architekten AG
MC# 5476-02
Weber.mur clima
Maxit, Saint-Gobain Weber
www.sg-weber.de

This wall plaster also incorporates PCMs to improve the insulative properties of the surface. Paraffin wax is used as the PCM, incorporated as encapsulated mini-spheres within the plaster. The spheres act as latent-heat storage materials that undergo a phase change at a specified temperature (from solid to liquid within the capsules). This property of the plaster allows for higher thermal storage mass without adding more weight to the construction. It is suitable only for interior wall surfaces.

ALTERSWOHNEN DOMAT/EMS
Dietrich Schwarz Architekten AG
MC# 6910-03
Policam Channeled Panels
(Multi-wall Polycarbonate Sheets)
Isık Plastik
www.isikplastik.com.tr

Even lighter than solid polycarbonate sheets, these multi-wall sheets are lightweight (less than one sixth that of glazing) and highly impact resistant. Though multiple channels reduce the overall transparency of the sheet, these panels can be processed with woodworking tools and bonded with compatible adhesives. They are used for high impact demand construction such as greenhouses, roofs, walkways, gymnasiums, and advertising sign panels.

NETHERLANDS INSTITUTE
FOR SOUND & VISION
Neutelings Riedijk Architects
MC# 6210-01
[vju:]
MEGALAB Bildkommunikation AG
www.megalab.com

These glass and photograph composite panels allow for permanent image bonding with the use of glazing. The photographs are fused between a cover glass and a special high-pressure laminate. The glass is scratch-resistant, anti-static, and easy to clean, and protects from dirt and moisture for decades. Used with specialty glass, this process is also suitable for glass floors and applications in wet areas.

NETHERLANDS INSTITUTE
FOR SOUND & VISION
Neutelings Riedijk Architects
MC# 6244-01
Rutschhemmender Siebdruck auf Glas
Joh. Sprinz GmbH & Co. KG
www.sprinz.eu

Glass is rarely used for flooring surfaces, as it is highly slippery when wet. This ceramic anti-slip coating is screen-printed onto laminated safety glass to significantly increase friction. Abrasion-resistant and easy to clean, it offers various grades of slip resistance depending on the slip hazard. The ceramic coating makes the glass translucent and various patterns can be screen-printed. It is used for interior and exterior walkable glazing such as stairs, floors, or pedestals.

NETHERLANDS INSTITUTE
FOR SOUND & VISION
Neutelings Riedijk Architects
MC# 6634-01
Ipachrome
Interpane Sicherheitsglas GmbH
www.interpane.com

This multilayer system for decorative glazing contains chromium and offers mirroring of glass that is significantly more robust than a conventional "silver" mirror. The chrome layer is printed on, offering filigree or other pattern effects, and, in addition, it can be combined with proprietary heat and sunscreen functions and processed to create insulated glass. The printed panels are used for interior and exterior applications, façade panels, and store and trade show construction.

YALE UNIVERSITY
SCULPTURE BUILDING & GALLERY
KieranTimberlake
MC# 4755-02
Pyrogel®
Aspen Aerogels®
www.aerogel.com

This flexible insulation blanket contains aerogel and is used for insulation at high temperatures. Silica-based aerogel particles are incorporated into a non-woven carbon- and glass-fiber batting blanket that is non-toxic, supple, low-dusting, and waterproof – ideal for wet environments. Used for insulation pipes, footwear, extreme weather apparel, boilers, and underground steam lines, the blanket has a maximum continuous service temperature of 385°C (725°F) and may be cut using conventional textile-cutting.

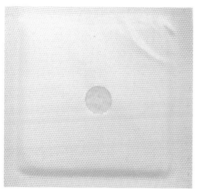

YALE UNIVERSITY
SCULPTURE BUILDING & GALLERY
KieranTimberlake
MC# 6912-01
Tensotherm™
Birdair, Inc.
www.tensothermroofing.com

This flexible, tensile roofing system incorporates aerogel particles within a thermal batting to increase thermal and sound insulation. The "padded fabric" is a translucent, lightweight multilayer insulation system used as a permanent roofing membrane for sporting, institutional, commercial, retail, and transportation structures. The system retains the functional benefits of a standard PTFE roofing material—lightweight, durable, and translucent with minimal maintenance—while improving heat insulation and acoustical dampening performance.

BAHA'I TEMPLE OF
SOUTH AMERICA
Hariri Pontarini Architects
MC# 5701-02
Glass Ore
Technical Glass Products
www.tgpamerica.com

Blurring the distinction between glass and ceramic, these fused-glass bricks have the durability and performance of ceramic and the size and heft of a brick. They are non-porous, have a milky white translucent appearance and are available in a standard 98.4 x 197 x 60.3 mm (3.875 x 7.75 x 2.375 in.). Each brick weighs 2.72 kg (6 lbs.). Applications are for interior or exterior wall cladding, furniture, or flooring.

BAHA'I TEMPLE OF
SOUTH AMERICA
Hariri Pontarini Architects
MC# 6154-01
Wellen–und Wabenglas
Willems GmbH gold-mosaics
www.gold-mosaics.com

This decorative, kiln-formed glass has honeycomb and wave patterns produced by fusing together shaped rods of glass at 900°C (1652°F). The honeycomb glass is made by fusing optical-glass rods and colorful ARTISTA glass. The first fusion result is polished by hand to create color gradients and then fire-polished in a furnace. The material is available in different colors (blue, green, amber, white) and with different finishes (polished, sandblasted, brushed). Applications include interior and exterior decoration, dividers, vanities, sinks, lighting, wall and floor tiles, and runways.

KILDEN PERFORMING ARTS CENTRE
ALA Architects
MC# 6919-01
BioWood
Green Resources Material Australia Pty Ltd
www.grmaustralia.com.au

Alternatives to wood have improved significantly in the last decade with various composite versions which combine wood fibers with small amounts of plastic as a binder. This version uses recycled PVC as the binder, much harder and more durable than the standard plastics typically used, offering a lower heat gain, greater scratch- and fire-resistance and will expand less with heat changes. Extruded into various forms of planks, it can be screwed, sawed and CNC routed much like regular wood and is hard to differentiate from the real thing.

VILLA WELPELOO
Superuse Studios
MC# 6685-01
Chylon
CHENNA SRL
www.chenna.it

There is an increasing number of recycled wood sources that combine fibers with recycled plastics. This wood–polymer composite (WPC) material is 55% recycled polyethylene (PE) and 45% recycled wood. The plastic content is recuperated from recycled containers, while the wood fiber is derived from leftover shavings from the processing of timber panels. This strong, rigid material has good anti-slip properties, is chemical-, water- and UV-resistant, and does not freeze or require maintenance. It is used as exterior cladding, decking, and as a replacement for MDF and OSB.

VILLA WELPELOO
Superuse Studios
MC# 6700-01
Aged Woods®
Aged Woods, Inc.
www.agedwoods.com

This reclaimed wood flooring has been re-milled from recycled wood from old disused barns. Various species include Bunkhouse Plank® Oak, Antique Distressed® Oak, Antique Distressed® White Pine, Bunkhouse Plank® Yellow Pine and Antique Maple. The timber is FSC-certified and contributes to LEED MR 4 (recycled content), MR 7 (certified wood), and EQ 4.4 (low-emitting materials).

CORK HOUSE
Arquitectos Anónimos
MC# 4571-04
Cork Artistico
Expanko, Ink
www.expanko.com

Cork remains a highly suitable interior flooring material thanks to its wear and water resistance and its insulative properties. There are both synthetic (water-based matte polyurethane) and natural (carnauba wax) finishes available for these cork tiles. Cork is the bark of the cork oak tree, a renewable resource harvested in nine-year cycles. The bark on the cork tree regenerates every nine years to an approximate thickness of 5–8 cm (2–3 in.). Harvesting of the cork does not damage the tree, and the trees will live up to 250 years.

CORK HOUSE
Arquitectos Anónimos
MC# 6384-03
Korkbaumrinde
Freund GmbH
www.freundgmbh.com

Unlike processed cork surfaces commonly seen as floor and wall tiles, these wall covering panels are made from directly harvested cork bark. The top layer consists of 100% natural raw material and displays the deep three-dimensional texture of the cork tree. The bark is laminated to a corkboard substrate, increasing formal stability. It is extremely lightweight and has good acoustic and thermal insulation properties, though with a lower wear resistance than standard processed cork. It is used as decoration and sound absorption on walls and ceilings in interior spaces.

CORK HOUSE
Arquitectos Anónimos
MC# 6841-01
Suberra
ECO Supply
www.ecosupplycenter.com

Despite reduced use of cork for wine bottles, there is a considerable amount of waste cork that can be usefully recycled. This surfacing material is composed of 100% post-industrial recycled cork pulp and compressed with polyurethane glue without the addition of formaldehyde. The closed-cell structure resists water and stains and naturally inhibits bacterial growth. The material has a class B fire rating with a resistance of up to 176°C (350°F).

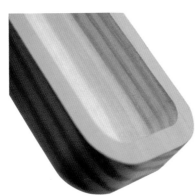

MENTAL HEALTH INSTITUTE GGZ-NIJMEGEN
BogermanDill
MC# 4780-08
Perennial Wood™
Eastman Chemical Company
www.eastman.com

Acetylation, the process of treating wood with a vinegar-like substance to harden and waterproof it, has been around since the 1930s but has only recently become economically viable. Leaving a slight vinegar smell after treatment, it enables softwoods to act as though they were durable hardwoods. This gives protection, even uncoated, against decades of outdoor exposure. Acetylation does not stop the wood being sawed, nailed, screwed or otherwise worked like any other lumber. There may, however, be a darkening in the color of the wood over time.

EARTH BRICKS
Atelier Tekuto
MC# 5152-01
Eco Cements
TecEco Pty Ltd
www.tececo.com

Cement production is one of the largest carbon emitters in construction. However, cements that contain large amounts of magnesia can actually remove carbon dioxide from the surrounding atmosphere. Mimicking nature, these Eco-Cement concretes absorb large amounts of CO_2 from the atmosphere in order to harden into cured cement. Other advantages are their potentially lower cost, carbon sequestration and waste utilization, and improved durability and performance. They are generally used for bricks, pavers, permeable pavements, and other porous cement-based products.

EARTH BRICKS
Atelier Tekuto
MC# 5995-01
Fly Ash Brick
EcologicTech
www.freightpipelinecompany.com

In an attempt to reduce the colossal carbon footprint of standard house bricks, this version is produced from 98% waste from coal power plants. Fly ash, a whitish powder left after coal is burned, is mixed with water then compacted at 4,000 psi in a steam bath. The mixture is then set into molds such as bricks, and sets as hard as concrete. The bricks pass standard tests for the material as well as withstanding 100 freeze-thaw cycles (tests require only 50). Its manufacturing uses significantly less energy and costs 20% less than standard house bricks.

EARTH BRICKS
Atelier Tekuto
MC# 6815-01

Tradical® Hemcrete®
American Lime Technology
www.americanlimetechnology.com

This biocomposite thermally insulating walling material made from hemp, lime and water is an alternative to concrete or cement blocks. It is considered "carbon negative" because the process of growing and harvesting the hemp captures and sequesters more atmospheric carbon dioxide than is generated during block manufacturing; approximately 100 m³ (3,530 ft³) of this building material locks up 155 tons of CO_2.

ONDA RESTAURANT
Alliance Arkitekter and MAPT
MC# 5606-01

Kebony 30
Kebony AS
www.kebony.com

This is a process for the weathering treatment of sustainable wood that incorporates naturally sourced, non-toxic chemicals. Biowaste, based on sugar cane and corn cob proteins, is forced into the cellular structure of the wood using pressure under vacuum, making it much more durable. The treated wood has better dimensional stability than untreated or preservative-treated wood. There is less shrinking and swelling when subjected to changes in humidity, and cracks are less likely to develop. It is mainly used for exterior construction projects in harsh environments.

ONDA RESTAURANT
Alliance Arkitekter and MAPT
MC# 6929-01

EcoClad
Klip BioTechnologies, Inc.
www.kliptech.com

This hard, durable cladding panel uses FSC-certified wood fiber from 33% post-consumer recycled paper, bamboo fiber and corn-and-cashew nut-based resin. A recycled, rapidly renewable alternative to vinyl and aluminum, it is almost impossible to crack, chip, or break under extreme weather conditions. It is highly scratch-resistant, with water absorption of less than 1%, and cannot be permanently stained from wine, bleach, grease, or acid. Certified by FSC and approved by SmartWood and the Rainforest Alliance, it contributes to LEED certification. Applications include interiors, exterior siding, soffits, and wainscoting.

STADTHAUS, MURRAY GROVE
Waugh Thistleton Architects
MC# 5842-02

Structure
e2e Materials
www.e2ematerials.com

This moldable biocomposite is manufactured utilizing a proprietary soy-based resin system and natural renewable fibers including jute, flax, and kenaf. It offers a stiffer, stronger, 66% lighter, flame-retardant alternative to thermoformed or otherwise molded plastic and can create complex shapes not possible with existing wood composites. It does not use petrochemicals, requires 60% less energy to create, contains zero formaldehyde, and is entirely biodegradable. It may be shaped by thermoforming to corrugated and textured panels and may be recycled, incinerated, or composted.

STADTHAUS, MURRAY GROVE
Waugh Thistleton Architects
MC# 6216-08

Translucent Wood
Lamellux®
www.lamellux.com

Creating a unique combination of timber structure and translucency, these light-transmitting panels are composed of glued wood strips with aligned optical fibers in between. Though not as strong as solid timber, they can be used in areas where less strength is needed, such as paneling, countertops, doors, partitions, and furniture. Various wood species are also offered: oak, beech, ash, sycamore, cherry, walnut, teak, African mahogany, bubinga, wenge, and zebra, with finishes of a satin varnish, stained, and others.

STADTHAUS, MURRAY GROVE
Waugh Thistleton Architects
MC# 6970-03

DendroLight® Building Block
Dendrolight Latvija Ltd
www.dendrolight.lv

Constructed with a cellular core layer sandwiched between solid wood or plywood blocks, this wood panel is half the weight of solid timber with high strength and good thermal and sound insulation. The middle layer is made from a selection of wood profiles, which are then glued together at perpendicular angles and sawed into sheets. The panel has low swelling characteristics, no internal tensions and high homogeneous surface stability. Applications include flooring, ceiling panels, internal and external wall elements, and roof panels.

PAVILION HERMÈS FOR
MILON DESIGN WEEK
**Shigeru Ban Architects / Jean de Gastines
Architectes**
MC# 5518-01
PaperStone®
PaperStone
www.paperstoneproducts.com

This solid surfacing panel has the performance of
Corian, but is made from 100% post-consumer
recycled paper. Waste paper pulp is mixed with a
water-based, non-petroleum phenolic resin with no
detectable formaldehyde to produce a rigid, hard,
durable solid surfacing sheet. The panels may be
worked much like hardwood. Certified by the FSC and
approved by SmartWood and the Rainforest Alliance,
the material contributes to LEED certification.
Applications include countertops, work surfaces,
tables, and backsplashes.

PAVILION HERMÈS FOR
MILAN DESIGN WEEK
**Shigeru Ban Architects / Jean de Gastines
Architectes**
MC# 6241-01
Krütex®
Krüger & Sohn GmbH
www.krueger-und-sohn.de

Impregnating cotton fabrics with phenolic resin can
produce composite profiles with amazing strength.
Rods, square and round tubes, sheets and formed
parts are made by layering cotton fabrics impregnated
with phenolic resin and glue under heat and pressure.
They are mainly used in machine construction but also
in the electronics industry as construction materials.
Another main field of usage is in hydraulic and bearing
productions.

PAVILION HERMÈS FOR
MILAN DESIGN WEEK
**Shigeru Ban Architects / Jean de Gastines
Architectes**
MC# 6560-05
Ecor®
ECOR - Noble Environmental Technologies
Corporation
www.ecorglobal.com

These 3D pressure-molded honeycomb panels with
edge banding are produced utilizing low-energy
processing techniques. They are comprised of agro-
fiber (including plant fibers and bovine processed
fibers) and post-consumer waste (old corrugated
cardboard, old newspaper, etc.). This creates a high-
strength, recyclable composite structure that can be
used for furniture and POP displays where edges
need to be smooth and uniform.

PAVILION HERMÈS FOR
MILAN DESIGN WEEK
**Shigeru Ban Architects / Jean de Gastines
Architectes**
MC# 6589-02
Paper derived from milk cartons
Paper World Corp
www.paperworld.jp

This paperboard is derived from recycled beverage
containers; the surface is recycled milk cartons and
other assorted beverage containers, while the middle
layer is made of recycled papers, such as newspapers
and magazines. It is used for packaging, but has the
strength for internal construction of furniture and
event design.

PAVILION HERMÈS FOR
MILAN DESIGN WEEK
**Shigeru Ban Architects / Jean de Gastines
Architectes**
MC# 6842-01
zBoard
Way Basics
www.waybasics.com

Using the stiffness and lightweight structure of
corrugated cardboard, this construction material system
is an alternative to particleboard, MDF, plywood, and
solid wood-based systems. It is made from 99% post-
consumer recycled paper and instead of mechanical
fasteners, a 3M brand adhesive tape is used to construct
the various products or units. Its internal structure gives
the material a strength and durability comparable to other
wood-engineered boards such as particleboard or MDF,
with lighter weight for the same thickness of panel.

COCOON_FS PAVILION
Pohl Architekten
MC# 4896-02
3Braid®
3TEX Incorporated
www.3tex.com

These braided preforms for composite manufacturing
utilize a braiding technique that creates 3D objects for
part production. Glass, carbon, and aramid fibers may
be braided using this process. Applications include
automotive racing and aerospace industries.

COCOON_FS PAVILION
Pohl Architekten
MC# 5323-04
Synlam
Cornerstone Research Group, Inc.
www.crgrp.com

To create lighter-weight composites, this manufacturer uses syntactic foams that incorporate incompressible glass microspheres to bulk up the profile without adding weight. The combination of this low-density filler with resin drastically reduces weight and maintains structural strength. Applications include aerospace airframes, architectural materials, boating and automotive parts, instrument housings, mirrors, space structures, and shelters.

COCOON_FS PAVILION
Pohl Architekten
MC# 6428-01
Curran®
Cellucomp
www.cellucomp.com

This natural fiber composite offers strength properties that are comparable to carbon fiber. A high-strength biofiber formulated from degraded carrots, it is produced by synthesis of degraded carrot fiber into nanostructured particulates that can be made into a coating. Currently used for a fishing rod that has better bending stiffness than a high-end carbon fiber competitor, coatings for carbon-fiber bikes and other sports equipment are in development. It also offers a very smooth, glossy finish and can be used as a top surface, for sporting goods, automotive, aerospace and consumer products.

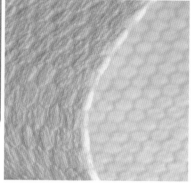

'MODULAR FABRICATION' STAND
UNStudio
MC# 2492-03
FR Soric®
Lantor BV
www.lantor.nl

This flame-retardant, flexible core material for lightweight composites is used in mass transit as well as in architecture. A halogen-free fire retardant is added to the manufacturer's core material, a polyester non-woven material with a compression-resistant hexagonal or random dot-printed cell structure. It is suited for use with vacuum infusion and resin transfer molding (RTM) processes for light composites to create complex shapes with lightweight cores.

'MODULAR FABRICATION' STAND
UNStudio
MC# 6733-01
barracuda®
Porcher Industries Groupe
www.porcher-ind.com

This aluminized glass-fiber fabric comes in multiple metallic colors and is an effective way of coloring composites without adding additional coatings. It can be used in vacuum forming, hand lay-up, resin transfer and autoclave molding. When combined with resin, finished parts maintain a silver sheen similar to formed steel and are strong, durable, and lightweight. They easily conform to irregular surfaces and, as such, applications include tennis rackets, helmets, kitchen appliances, luggage, and automotive parts.

ERICK VAN EGERAAT OFFICE TOWER
Designed by Erick van Egeraat
MC# 2492-04
Coremat XM
Lantor BV
www.lantor.nl

Less resin means less weight per part. This polyester non-woven fabric exhibits improved conformability for complex parts with lower resin usage while still maintaining strength. It is compatible for use with all regular types of resins including polyester, vinylester, phenolic, and epoxy. These membranes are currently used in marine areas (hulls, decks, and superstructures of boats and yachts), transportation (parts and panels of cars, trailers, and trucks), mass transit (interior and exterior of trains and buses), kayaks, surfboards, pools, and tubs.

ERICK VAN EGERAAT OFFICE TOWER
Designed by Erick van Egeraat
MC# 6138-02
TeXtreme Spread Tow Fabrics
Oxeon AB
www.oxeon.se

This carbon-fiber reinforcement utilizes a very flat structure to reduce the bulkiness of the preform. The fabric is based on the company's TapeWeaving technology, which uses tapes instead of yarn and can provide lower areal weights. In any given area more fibers can be packed in tape form than in yarn form. The fabrics are used in aerospace, automotive (sports car bodies), sporting goods (bicycle frames), and industrial applications (wind turbine blades).

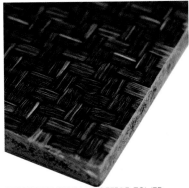

ERICK VAN EGERAAT OFFICE TOWER
Designed by Erick van Egeraat
MC# 6524-02
Vario Line® Sandwich Composites
PolymerPark Materials GmbH
www.polymer-park.com

These robust thermoplastic composite panels have a good ratio between weight, mechanical properties, and cost. Depending on the version, the panels are especially stiff or impact-resistant, but always lightweight, weather-resistant, low maintenance, and abrasion-proof. They can be mechanically processed by sawing, milling, nailing, screwing, and riveting, and can also be connected to each other. Applications include elements and floors for commercial vehicles and horse trailers as well as skateboard ramps and concrete switchboards.

HALLEY VI RESEARCH STATION
Hugh Broughton Architects
MC# 0426-02
WaveMax® 6000
Norplex-Micarta
www.norplex-micarta.com

This glass-fiber composite panel has the advantage of very high temperature resistance, while maintaining excellent machinability. They can be used to create strong but very thin walls without risk of breakout. It has excellent mechanical strength at a continuous operating temperature of 315°C (600°F) and can withstand short exposures to temperatures approaching 360°C (680°F). Applications include electronics (solder boards), construction (building panels), and aerospace (insulation for disc brakes).

HALLEY VI RESEARCH STATION
Hugh Broughton Architects
MC# 5835-01
Celstran
Celanese
www.ticona.com

These long-fiber-reinforced thermoplastics (LFRT) are produced by pultrusion technology. A variety of long fibers including glass fibers, stainless steel, carbon, aramid or other reinforcing fibers are fully impregnated to form an internal fiber "skeleton" that can then be molded. Conventional plastic forming methods such as injection molding, blow molding, rotocasting, and profile extrusion are possible with LFRT products. Applications include tool housings, luggage racks, fan shrouds, wheels, and gears.

HALLEY VI RESEARCH STATION
Hugh Broughton Architects
MC# 6690-01
Lamilux Antislip
Lamilux, Heinrich Strunz Group
www.lamilux.de

This fiberglass-reinforced laminate combines the mechanical properties and durability of fiberglass-reinforced composites with an anti-slip property. It is available as yard-ware or as sheet and in a wide range of colors. It is fire-rated, food-safe, and finds applications in commercial vehicles, loading areas, and loading ramps.

[C]SPACE PAVILION
Alan Dempsey and Alvin Huang
MC# 5232-01
Vubonite
Symbion N.V.
www.vubonite.com

Geopolymer compounds have the high temperature resistance of ceramics and the processability of polymers. Based on alumino-silicates and available as sheets, they are processed in a similar way to FRP (fiber-reinforced polymer composites), by pouring the geopolymer onto woven layers of ceramic or glass reinforcement. The compound is then cured at 80°C (176°F), as opposed to over 1,000°C (1,832°F) for ceramic firing. The cured compound withstands heat of up to 1200°C (2,192°F), and can be further reinforced using various inorganic fiber fillers and particulates.

[C]SPACE PAVILION
Alan Dempsey and Alvin Huang
MC# 6621-02
Faserzement naturerhrtet
Eternit AG
www.eternit.de

Fiber cement panels offer a cost-effective and inert façade material for exterior applications. These naturally cured fiber cement panels consist of fiber-reinforced cement stone that is dimensionally stable and weatherproof after it has been cured. The material consists of 40% Portland cement, 11% trass (a gray or cream-colored volcanic ash), 5% cellulose, 30% microscopic air voids, and 12% water. Synthetic fibers made from polyvinyl alcohol are used as fiber reinforcement. The panels are flame-resistant and UV-resistant and have a colorfast surface.

[C]SPACE PAVILION
Alan Dempsey and Alvin Huang
MC# 6847-02
Eter-Color
Eastern Architectural Products, LLC
www.fibercementproducts.com

This fiber cement panel is through-colored and exhibits natural variations and color hues throughout. It is non-combustible, sound-insulating, resistant to extreme temperatures, water, many living organisms and chemicals, and environmentally friendly, as it does not emit harmful gases. A strong and rigid sheet with a smooth aesthetic surface, applications include exterior façades and interior cladding applications for a broad spectrum of building types.

LILLE MÉTROPOLE MUSEUM
OF MODERN ART
Manuelle Gautrand Architecture
MC# 5058-09
Pixa™
Sensitile Systems
www.sensitile.com

This light-filtering panel is composed of a concrete substrate integrated with transparent acrylic light-conducting channels, and is a simplified, more graphic alternative to light-transmitting concrete. The material is available as slabs and tiles in seven different simple graphic patterns. A variety of standard cement colors are available in solid or speckled; and customization of shapes, arrangement of acrylic channels, and edge finishing for furniture and countertop applications are possible. It is available in both semi-gloss and ultra-high-gloss urethane finishes.

LILLE MÉTROPOLE MUSEUM
OF MODERN ART
Manuelle Gautrand Architecture
MC# 6242-01
I-Crete
iCrete, LLC
www.icrete.com

The exact composition, pouring and curing method of concrete can significantly affect its performance. This software system provides concrete producers with concrete mix designs and a production methodology that is able to increase the strength of the material up to 14,000 psi by determining the most effective type and composition of the concrete constituents. This process enables a reduction in material use of both concrete and reinforcing steel and a decrease of up to 40% in greenhouse gas emissions compared to standard poured concrete.

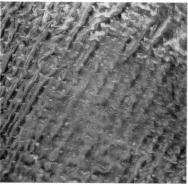

LILLE MÉTROPOLE MUSEUM
OF MODERN ART
Manuelle Gautrand Architecture
MC# 6421-02
Lucem
LUCEM GmbH
www.robatex.de

These pre-cast concrete "light-transmitting" panels incorporate glass fibers to impart translucency and can be cast into various forms as cladding, bricks, washbasins, and other shaped elements for both interior and exterior use. For the execution of translucent exterior walls, the bricks can be combined with a transparent insulation and a weather-protective layer of glass. The material is used for countertops, exterior walls, stairs, and landscaping elements.

LILLE MÉTROPOLE MUSEUM
OF MODERN ART
Manuelle Gautrand Architecture
MC# 6479-01
Concrete Cloth™ (CC)
Concrete Canvas Ltd (UK)
www.concretecanvas.co.uk

These cement-impregnated flexible fabrics harden on addition of water to form a thin, durable, waterproof and fireproof concrete layer. This "concrete cloth" is composed of a concrete blend and synthetic fibers with a clear PVC backing that ensures the material is waterproof, while hydrophilic fibers on the opposite surface aid hydration by drawing water into the cement. When water is added the material is flexible for two hours, then sets rapidly. Unset, the material is flexible and easily cut to shape, nailed or stapled, and fixed into complex curvatures using basic fixings.

STEDELIJK MUSEUM
Benthem Crouwel Architects
MC# 1254-03
QISO™ Triaxial Braiding
A&P Technology
www.braider.com

Triaxial woven composites reduce the potential weaknesses of many composites by spreading the load-bearing capabilities over the entire 360° range. Increasing the number of fiber directions from two to three and changing the orientation of the fibers increases the damage tolerance, while improving energy absorption. Multiple layers of the fabric reduce interlaminar stress. Applications include composite reinforcement in aerospace, engineering, sports equipment, and automotive racing, but they can be used anywhere composites are used.

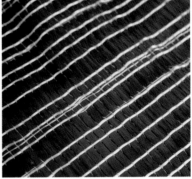

STEDELIJK MUSEUM
Benthem Crouwel Architects
MC# 4569-01
Vitech
Carr Reinforcements Ltd
www.carrreinforcements.com

Enabling woven Kevlar and carbon fiber fabrics to be effectively used as apparel, these tapes have been coated with a clear PVC or polyurethane laminate that has been bonded to the fabric using a binder. They are ideal for wear and impact resistance; two coating grades are for "soft" (glove components and body armor) and "hard" (motorcycle boots and rally car mud-flaps). The fabrics may be vacuum-molded to complex shapes and are typically used in the motorcycle apparel industry, but also find application in other industries.

STEDELIJK MUSEUM
Benthem Crouwel Architects
MC# 6354-01
Gummi-Faserverbundkunststoffe Direktverbund
Gummiwerk Kraiburg GmbH & Co. KG
www.kraiburg-kautschuk.de

This versatile combination of rubber and fiber-reinforced synthetic materials gives stiff and flexible sections on the same part. The rubber forms a direct bond with carbon fiber or glass-fiber composite. The material can be individually configured to reduce vibration, improve component protection, surface grip, surface feel, shatter resistance (a problem with carbon-fiber composites), and elasticity. Applications are for the automotive and aerospace industries, mechanical engineering, sports equipment, and medical engineering.

STEDELIJK MUSEUM
Benthem Crouwel Architects
MC# 6780-01
Multi-Axial Multi-Ply Fabric
SGL Kümpers, a member of SGL Group
www.sglgroup.com

Currently the thinnest carbon-fiber reinforcement available, its construction utilizes a very flat profile using carbon tape instead of yarn. In any given area more fibers can be packed in tape form than in a yarn. A woven material comprising interlacing fibrous tapes, instead of yarns, displays a substantially reduced number of interstices and openings. The fabrics are used in aerospace, automotive (sports car bodies), sporting goods (bicycle frames), and industrial applications (wind turbine blades).

ORANGE CUBE
Jakob + Macfarlane Architects
MC# 5406-01
Perforated Metal Sheet
Bergmann Hillebrand GmbH & Co. KG
www.bergmannhillebrand.de

High precision, perforated sheet metal that may be used for finished or semi-finished surfaces. The steel, stainless steel and aluminum sheets may also be formed, surface-textured, painted, or anodized according to specifications. Applications include speaker grilles, display stands, computer housings, light fixtures, ceiling panels, and other consumer product and interior accent purposes.

ORANGE CUBE
Jakob + Macfarlane Architects
MC# 5492-01
Mevacovario
Mevaco GmbH
www.mevaco.com

These custom-perforated metal sheets are suitable for a wide range of applications. Aluminum, plain carbon and stainless steel, titanium zinc or brass sheets are perforated with round or square holes in any pattern or size. The sheets can be non-perforated in specific sections to ensure suitable strength, and may be cut, folded, welded, or curved. Applications include architectural, automotive, interior, and consumer products.

ORANGE CUBE
Jakob + Macfarlane Architects
MC# 6309-01
Dynamicwall
Easycom & Co. S.r.l.
www.dynamicwall.it

This digitally printed metal mesh is made from an aluminum sheet that is perforated and printed with any digital image to a maximum individual sheet size of 1500 x 3500 mm (60 x 137.8 in.). The panels can be combined to create a larger print size or bent, curved, cut, and welded like aluminum, while keeping the image water- and UV-resistant. Compliant with European standards for exterior surfaces, applications include exterior wall surfaces, decorative pieces and sculptures as well as interior partitions and ceilings.

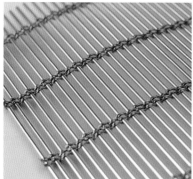

41 COOPER SQUARE
Morphosis Architects
MC# 1437-06
Lago
GKD-USA, Inc.
www.gkdmetalfabrics.com

This stainless steel woven mesh combines flexible drawn steel wire and rigid thin bars to give flexibility in only one direction. 44% is open area and it is used externally for façades, wall coverings, ceilings, gates, sunshades, displays, and exhibition stands.

41 COOPER SQUARE
Morphosis Architects
MC# 5588-02
Sheer Metal with Trevira CS backing
Sophie Mallebranche / Material Design Group
www.sophiemallebranche.com

Taking metal wire weaving to an artistic level, these custom-designed metal textiles are woven with 316L stainless steel micro-rope (warp) and stainless steel monofilament (weft) or silver-coated enameled copper monofilament (weft). The resulting fabrics have flexibility in the long (warp) direction. These textiles have been used as sculptural drapery for Chanel, Guerlain, Dior Perfumes, Hermès, Louis Vuitton, Ritz Carlton and specifiers for high-end residential projects. Applications include window and wall coverings.

41 COOPER SQUARE
Morphosis Architects
MC# 5946-06
Golf Sierra Small
Twentinox
www.twentinox.com

Architectural mesh fabric offers the security and durability of perforated metals, but with greater flexibility and variation in design and material. For this version, either round or flat spiral wire is woven on corrugated pins and then welded at the edges to create a durable mesh fabric. Custom designs are possible per request, and its open area is roughly 78%. Applications are for wall and ceiling coverings, room dividers, wire cloth façades (interior and exterior), and sunscreens.

41 COOPER SQUARE
Morphosis Architects
MC# 6557-02
Stainless Steel Wire Mesh
Thai Prasit Textile Company
www.thailandmesh.com

Using standard weaving techniques to create a semi-flexible steel sheet, variation of the wire diameter and weave construction can create a range of different appearances and performances. It is used for filtration of oils, chemicals, food, pharmaceuticals, and in petrochemical processes. It is also used as an insect screen for windows and doors and can be custom-cut into finished goods.

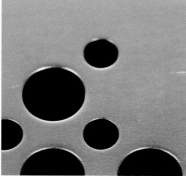

41 COOPER SQUARE
Morphosis Architects
MC# 6991-01
Perfor-Art®
Ishikawa Wire Netting Co., Ltd
www.ishikawa-kanaami.com

The combination of small and large punched holes and embedded silicone rubber pieces in these perforated panels creates a degree of realism unattainable in conventional perforation methods. The pattern can also be chosen to reduce window noise, a problem for high-rise buildings. It can be used to create symbols, logos, illustrations, scenery, and images of people. Potential uses include exterior fences, shutters, light fixtures, or railings; interior furniture, walls or display panels; and signage.

ORDOS ART & CITY MUSEUM
MAD Architects
MC# 0247-02
Impression™
Forms+Surfaces
www.forms-surfaces.com

These exterior architectural metal sheets are offered in a range of textures, including work-hardened surfaces, random abrasion, bead-blasted finishes, and satin finishes; flat and pre-curved panels may also be ordered. The panels are used for interior architectural cladding for walls, columns, trim, wainscoting, door panels, and elevator interiors.

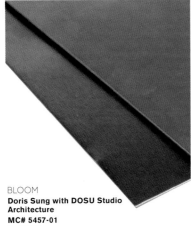

BLOOM
Doris Sung with DOSU Studio Architecture
MC# 5457-01
Cu/Al/Ni
Wickeder Westfalenstahl GmbH
www.wickeder.de

These bimetallic strips (foils) incorporate two different metals that are bonded together to allow for a protective outer layer (copper) with a less expensive inner core material (steel). This combination of two metals, typically steel, stainless steel, non-ferrous metals and copper can be used predominantly in cookware. However, their applications also include bimetallic strips for automotive, electronics, and battery parts. The metals are first cleaned and then bonded together between two rollers and can be deep-drawn, formed, or welded.

BLOOM
Doris Sung with DOSU Studio Architecture
MC# 5519-01
Borit®
Borit Leichtbau-Technik GmbH
www.borit.de

Bonding metals together can significantly increase their rigidity. In addition, these metal sheets utilize indentations to impart further stiffness. Two metal sheets, of stainless steel, copper, titanium, zinc, zinc-coated steel or magnesium, are hydroformed with regular square forms or other shapes. These sheets are staggered and glued together back-to-back to create a very stiff sheet. The top and bottom faces can then be laminated with a decorative sheet. Applications include dividing panels, work surfaces, electromagnetic shielding, and furniture design.

SOUMAYA MUSEUM
FR-EE Fernando Romero Enterprise
MC# 1627-08
DIBOND® Stucco
3A Composites
www.3acomposites.com

This aluminum composite panel has a distinctive finish, combining the uneven raised texture of traditional stucco plaster with a highly reflective surface. A special aluminum cover layer that is anodized after embossing gives a surface that is extremely hardwearing and conforms to food-grade material specifications. The surface is highly tactile and resistant to marking, making it suitable for high traffic areas. Typical applications include bars and counters, fasciae and wall finishes, furniture and displays.

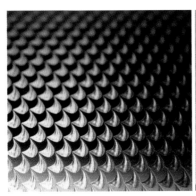

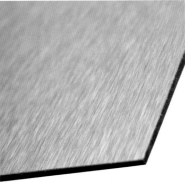

SOUMAYA MUSEUM
FR-EE Fernando Romero Enterprise
MC# 6249-01
Aluminium-Zierelemente
Faurecia Angell-Demmel
www.faurecia.de

This process custom-forms metals such as aluminum, titanium steel, and pewter, and combines color high-resolution printing, various gloss levels, introduction of textural elements and structures as well as various metallic effects such as brushing. Functional processes add custom properties to the product surfaces be it weatherability, shock, impact or scratch resistance. Different metals in combination with each other can be processed. Applications are for custom metal surfaces for automotive parts, consumer products, and interior architectural details.

SOUMAYA MUSEUM
FR-EE Fernando Romero Enterprise
MC# 6793-01
Tosolbond®
Tosolbond Composites LLC
www.tosolbond.com

The combination of aluminum exterior sheets and a low-density polyethylene (non-combustible mineral-filled) core gives these panels sound and vibration absorption, easy workability, and the ability to create living hinges and effective folding geometries. It is typically used as flat or curved panels for exterior and interior cladding and roof covering, on new buildings and retrofit applications.

'LABRYS FRISAE'
THEVERYMANY
MC# 6833-01
Micralox
Sanford Process Corporation
www.micralox.com

Aluminum anodizing processes are normally unable to offer a full range of colors as well as suitable corrosion resistance and weathering durability for exterior architecture. This version, however, incorporates a micro-crystalline barrier surface that offers much greater resistance to corrosive environments. This organization at the micro- and nano-scale directly results in a superior coating and protection of the underlining aluminum material. This coating has increased resistance to wear and chemical corrosion and eliminates color fading even when exposed to superheated steam.

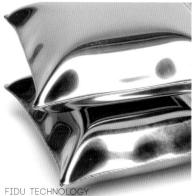

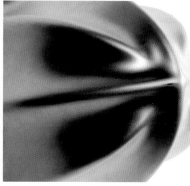

FIDU TECHNOLOGY
Zieta Prozessdesign
MC# 5368-01
Blown Metal Shapes
fullblown metals
www.stephennewby.co.uk

This process for inflating metal shapes using high pressure mimics the FiDU process developed by Oscar Zieta. Two matching squares of metal such as steel or aluminum are welded at the edges and then inflated to create a pillow effect. The resulting form maintains its shape and has good structural strength. It is possible to use this process with a range of simple shapes, though size is limited. This process is mainly used in the production of decorative objects.

FIDU TECHNOLOGY
Zieta Prozessdesign
MC# 5797-01
Hydroforming
HMT Technologie und Handel Gmbh
www.hmt.co.at

This cost-efficient hydromechanical deep-drawing process is used for the plastic forming of flat sheet metal into cylindrical, conical, or parabolic hollow parts. This tension-pressure-pressure combination increases the plasticizing capability of the material and enables the creation of highly complex forms out of basically any ductile metal. The advantages of this process are that the parts can be produced in a single deep-drawing process, that no drawing beads or drawing marks occur, and that the raw material for deep-drawn components can already be coated, lacquered, or polished.

FIDU TECHNOLOGY
Zieta Prozessdesign
MC# 6800-01
Industrial Origami®
Industrial Origami Inc.
www.industrialorigami.com

Industrial Origami is a metal-forming stamping process for aluminum and steel alloys, similar to current perforated cardboard folding. This process creates fatigue "lances" in metal that allow highly accurate, complex shapes to be easily folded with low force and the formation of stronger, higher fatigue-resistant, load-bearing assemblies that significantly reduce welding and fastening. They are also designed to maintain optimal edge-to-face engagement for high-tensile-strength materials. Applications are found in the construction, automotive, furniture, appliance, and substrate industries.

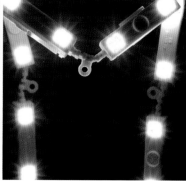

EAST BEACH CAFÉ
Heatherwick Studio
MC# 5085-01
Tecu® Copper Cladding
KME
www.kme.com

This simple architectural cladding is based on copper sheets designed to acquire a patina. Phosphorus deoxidized copper sheet is used for a wide range of construction façades, and is available in sheets, strips, shingles, and nets. Due to the nature of copper, it is susceptible to small amounts of corrosion, developing a matte dark-brown coloring from weather and oxidation. In addition to the untreated surface, there are three other finishes available: Patina; Oxid, a pre-oxidized dark-brown coating; and Zinn, a zinc-coated copper sheet.

EAST BEACH CAFÉ
Heatherwick Studio
MC# 6543-01
Pigmento® Red
Umicore
www.vmzinc.com

Zinc has the ability to take on a patina of various subtle color variations. This material is a zinc–titanium alloy treated to obtain a pre-weathered surface with the appearance and texture of a natural patina. The surface treatment modifies the top 1 micron (0.001 mm) of the material to produce a corrosion- and abrasion-resistant finish. The surface finish is "self-healing," meaning that scratches introduced during installation or wear will be "healed" by the formation of a natural patina. The lifetime of zinc-titanium roofing material is greater than 100 years.

ALLIANZ ARENA
Herzog & de Meuron
MC# 5805-05
Tetra® MAX
GE Lighting Solutions
www.gelightingsolutions.com

Flexible strands of LEDs that offer increased brightness. These lights can be installed in curved patterns or on curved surfaces, require low voltages and produce little heat. The LEDs are available in red, red-orange, goldenrod, green, aquamarine, sky blue, blue, and white. Currently, these lights are used in architectural signage, accent lighting, and canopy lighting.

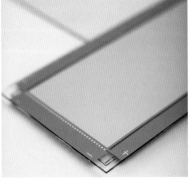

ALLIANZ ARENA
Herzog & de Meuron
MC# 6561-01
Lumisys™
Top Nanosys Inc.
www.topnanosys.com

This transparent flexible polymer sheet incorporates working LED lights. The polymer film is coated with a transparent, thin layer of carbon nanotubes in a specific configuration that acts like wiring to connect the LED lights. A protective clear film is then applied on top to insulate the conductive circuit. This type of conductive film is an alternative to ITO (indium tin oxide) coatings used in other transparent LED films, offering a more efficient and lower-cost process for producing this type of film. Applications include housewares, portable electronics, and automotive.

ALLIANZ ARENA
Herzog & de Meuron
MC# 6727-01
Philips Lumiblade
Philips Technologie GmbH
www.lumiblade.com

Based on organic LEDs, this extremely thin light source emits from its entire surface and exhibits diffuse radiating characteristics. It consists of glass and very thin layers of aluminum, ITO (indium tin oxide), and hydrocarbon. When switched off, the module acts as a mirror. Applications are found in interior design, aesthetic light accents, advertising, and mood lighting.

OLYMPIC SHOOTING VENUE
Magma Architecture
MC# 5933-01
PVDF II Series
Hiraoka & Co., Ltd
www.tarpo-hiraoka.com

These wide format coated fabrics for exterior architectural applications use a Polyvinylidene fluoride (PVDF) top coating to make it more dirt resistant and to maintain a whiter appearance after extended sun exposure. The underlying fabric is a central woven polyester scrim, with an acrylic lacquer layer, and a polyvinyl chloride (PVC) top layer and another acrylic lacquer layer. The fabrics have excellent soiling resistance, are easy to clean and do not require abrasion work before welding of the seams, which is typical of PTFE (Teflon) coated fabrics.

MEDIA-ICT
Cloud 9
MC# 5210-06
SEFAR® Architecture I / E-200-S
Sefar AG
www.sefar.com

100% Polyvinylidene fluoride (PVDF) mesh that is used in vertical façade applications. This mesh is similar to PTFE in durability—it is UV-resistant, colorfast, weatherproof, dirt- and water-repellent, and does not absorb moisture. It has a ten-year replacement warranty and a twenty-year expected lifespan. It can be sewn together and supported by a clamping system for easy installation. Applications are for vertical façade covers and shade protection, overhead shade protection, and lighter-weight replacement for metal mesh used as a vertical façade.

MEDIA-ICT
Cloud 9
MC# 6779-01
Power Plastic
Konarka Technologies, Inc.
www.konarka.com

These solar panels consisting of photoreactive materials are the next generation of photovoltaic technology, made from conductive polymers and organic nano-engineered materials. They can be printed or coated onto flexible plastic using an inexpensive, energy-efficient patented manufacturing process. They are suitable for outdoor use and, though not yet as efficient as some of the silicon-based solar panels, can be printed onto large surfaces in much the same way that signage is currently produced.

COCA-COLA BEATBOX PAVILION
Pernilla & Asif
MC# 5019-02
Vikuiti™
3M Optical Systems Division
www.vikuiti.com

To reduce glare and reflection, this polymer film has anti-glare properties for use in rear-projection screens. The film is a polarizing filter that may be applied to glass or other plastics to increase contrast, decrease reflectivity, and reduce glare. Two versions are available: one for light control, the other for anti-reflection. It can also be used to reduce unwanted reflections from windows as well as in other non-display applications. Typical applications are for films on flat panel displays, CRTs, LCDs, and touch screens.

COCA-COLA BEATBOX PAVILION
Pernilla & Asif
MC# 5210-05
SEFAR® Exterior Line
Sefar AG
www.sefar.com

These architectural fabrics are constructed from polytetrafluoroethylene (PTFE) scrim with a fluoropolymer (PTFE family) coating. The product is UV-resistant, colorfast, weatherproof, dirt- and water-repellent, and does not absorb moisture. The white fabrics are available with light transmission rates ranging from 35% to 65% and are suitable for both interior and exterior applications, such as membrane and lamellar structures, sun blinds, screens, awnings, luminous ceilings and walls, and projection surfaces.

COCA-COLA BEATBOX PAVILION
Pernilla & Asif
MC# 6550-02
InCycle®
MicroGREEN Polymers, Inc.
www.microgreeninc.com

These expanded thermoplastic polymer sheets use virgin, blended, or recycled polyester (PET) to create lightweight, printable, foldable, and formable sheets using proprietary Ad-Air technology to create a microcellular bubble structure that increases the entire roll by about 150% in width and length and 200% in thickness and reduces density by as much as 20%. FDA-compliant, the sheets have superior thermal insulation, and are grease- and waterproof. Applications include food and beverage, electronics, appliances, building materials, and packaging.

KHAN SHATYR ENTERTAINMENT CENTRE
Foster + Partners
MC# 3487-01
Texlon®
Vector Foiltec
www.vector-foiltec.com

Invented 30 years ago, Texlon—a "climatic envelope"— is still at the forefront of architectural innovation. Ethylene tetrafluoroethylene (ETFE) is the transparent, tear and weather resistant film that is the go-to solution for these transparent membranes, and offers such incredible reductions in weight compared to glass that it redefines what is possible with these structures. The film is also air tight, enabling the creation of multiple "envelopes" for added heat insulation.

KHAN SHATYR ENTERTAINMENT CENTRE
Foster + Partners
MC# 5963-01
Flexible Heating film
thermo Heating Elements LLC
www.thermo-llc.com

As a way of ensuring low condensation and maintaining an ambient temperature on polymer films, they can be heated using printed heating lines. This range of thin, flexible heating surfaces is deposited by screen-printing. Various types are available that are flexible, clear, temperature regulating, and suitable for wet environments. Applications for these heaters are found in the automotive (defogging of rear-view mirrors), medical (blood bottle storage), and manufacturing (tempering milking stations) industries.

KHAN SHATYR ENTERTAINMENT CENTRE
Foster + Partners
MC# 6598-01
Aculon
Aculon
www.aculon.com

For polymer films that are not naturally hydrophobic (where water beads up and rolls off), a coating can be applied to ensure resistance to dirt. Aculon is a high-performance hydrophobic and oleophobic (oil-resistant) coating for metal, glass, and polymer surfaces. The transparent coating has a surface that is slippery and smooth to the touch. The coating material is permanently bonded to the substrate in ambient conditions and does not leach from the substrate. Applications include eyeglasses, flat panel displays, and stainless steel, as well as for polymer films.

AIA PAVILION
Gernot Riether / Digital Fabrication Laboratory, Georgia Institute of Technology
MC# 4811-01
Air-cushion roofs
Buitink Technology
www.buitink-technology.com

Beyond the use of ETFE as a transparent membrane, Buitink Technology has pioneered the use of these films for use as "air cushion roofs," creating architectural structures that use panels constructed using ETFE, inflated by air to give structure and insulation. Because the films are easily printable, silver inks are used to add heat reflection, further enhancing their climatic control performance.

RESOURCES

Professional Organizations

American Architectural Foundation
1020 19th Street NW, Suite 525
Washington, DC 20036
United States
T: 1 202 787 1001
E: info@archfoundation.org
www.archfoundation.org

The American Institute of Architects (AIA)
1735 New York Avenue NW
Washington, DC 20006-5292
United States
T: 1 800 AIA 3837
E: infocentral@aia.org
www.aia.org

The Architects' Council of Europe
29 rue Paul Emile Janson
1050 Brussels
Belgium
T: 32 2 543 1140
www.ace-cae.org

Architectural Research Centers
Consortium (ARCC)
www.arccweb.org

Architectural Society of China (ASC)
No. 9 Sanlihe Road
Zicheng District, Beijing 100835
China
T: 86 010 88082227
F: 86 010 88082224
E: asc@mail.cin.gov.cn
www.chinaasc.org

The Japan Institute of Architects (JIA)
Hall 2-3-18JIA Jingumae, Shibuya-ku
Tokyo 150-0001
Japan
T: 03 3408 7125
F: 03 3408 7129
www.jia.or.jp

The Royal Institute of British Architects
(RIBA)
66 Portland Place
London W1B 1AD
United Kingdom
T: 44 20 7580 5533
www.architecture.com

Trade Shows and Events

JANUARY

Internationale Möbelmesse (IMM)
Cologne
www.imm-cologne.com

Maison & Objet
www.maison-objet.com

MARCH

Architectural Research Centers
Consortium (ARCC) Annual Conference
www.arccweb.org

Association of Collegiate Schools of
Architecture (ACSA) Annual Meeting
www.acsa-arch.org/programs-events/
conferences

APRIL

Global Shop, sponsored by the
Association for Retail Environments
(ARE)
www.globalshop.org

Milan Furniture Fair / Salone
Internazionale del Mobile
www.cosmit.it

MAY

HD Expo / Hospitality Design
Exposition and Conference
www.hdexpo.com

International Contemporary Furniture Fair
www.icff.com

JUNE

The American Institute of Architects
(AIA) National Convention
www.aia.org

The International Venice Biennale /
La Biennale di Venezia
www.labiennale.org/en/architecture

NeoCon
www.neocon.com

SEPTEMBER

100% Design / The London Design
Festival
www.100percentdesign.co.uk

Materials Research Websites

The Building Materials Reuse
Association
www.bmra.org

CORE-Materials / Collaborative Open
Resource Environment for Materials
www.core.materials.ac.uk

Institute of Materials, Minerals and
Mining (IOM3) – Materials resources for
students in building industries
www.iom3.org

Material Lab at the University of Texas
at Austin School of Architecture
www.soa.utexas.edu/matlab

Transmaterial
www.transmaterial.net

U.S. Green Building Council
www.usgbc.org

Networks for Architects

ArchiExpo
www.archiexpo.com

Archinect
www.archinect.com

Dexigner
www.dexigner.com

modeLab
www.lab.modecollective.nu

Open Architecture Network
www.openarchitecturenetwork.org

Blogs

An-Architecture
www.an-architecture.com

Architechnophilia
www.architechnophilia.blogspot.com

Architerials
www.architerials.com

Architizer
www.architizer.com

BLDG Blog
www.bldgblog.blogspot.com

Composites and Architecture
www.compositesandarchitecture.com

Cool Hunting
www.coolhunting.com

A Daily Dose of Architecture
www.archidose.blogspot.com

Death by Architecture
www.deathbyarchitecture.com

Jetson Green
www.jetsongreen.com

Plethora Project
www.plethora-project.com

Pruned
www.pruned.blogspot.com

Magazines (Digital and Print)

Arch Daily
www.archdaily.com

The Architects Newspaper
www.archpaper.com

Architectural Record
www.archrecord.construction.com

ArchitectureLab
www.architecturelab.net

Architype Review
www.architypereview.com

ArchNewsNow
www.archnewsnow.com

Azure
www.azuremagazine.com

Conditions Magazine
www.conditionsmagazine.com

Core77
www.core77.com

designboom
www.designboom.com

Design Bureau
www.wearedesignbureau.com

design milk
www.design-milk.com

Design Observer
www.designobserver.com

Detail
www.detail-online.com

Dezeen
www.dezeen.com

Domus
www.domusweb.it

eOculus – the American Institute of
Architects, New York
www.aiany.org/eOCULUS/newsletter

Icon Eye
www.iconeye.com

Metropolis
www.metropolismag.com

MoCo Loco
www.mocoloco.com

Surface
www.surfacemag.com

Treehugger
www.treehugger.com

Wallpaper
www.wallpaper.com

World Architecture News
www.worldarchitecturenews.com

ADDITIONAL READING

Addington, Michelle and Daniel L. Schodek. *Smart Materials and New Technologies: for the Architecture and Design Professions*. Architectural Press, Amsterdam, Boston and London, 2005

Allen, Edward and Joseph Iano. *Fundamentals of Building Construction: Materials and Methods*. Wiley, Hoboken, 2008

Ashby, Michael F. *Materials and the Environment,* Second edition: *Eco-informed Material Choice*. Butterworth-Heinemann, Amsterdam and Boston, 2012

Bahamón, Alejandro and Maria Camila Sanjinés. *Rematerial: From Waste to Architecture*. W. W. Norton & Co., New York, 2010

Bell, Michael and Craig Buckley. *Post-Ductility: Metals in Architecture and Engineering (Columbia Books on Architecture, Engineering, and Materials)*. Princeton Architectural Press, New York, 2012

Bell, Michael and Craig Buckley. *Solid States: Concrete in Transition (Columbia Books on Architecture, Engineering, and Materials)*. Princeton Architectural Press, New York, 2010

Bell, Michael and Jeannie Kim. *Engineered Transparency: the Technical, Visual, and Spatial Effects of Glass*. Princeton Architectural Press, New York, 2008

Bell, Victoria Ballard and Patrick Rand. *Materials for Design*. Princeton Architectural Press, New York, 2006

Beylerian, George M., Andrew Dent and Anita Moryadas. *Material ConneXion: The Global Resource of New and Innovative Materials for Architects, Artists, and Designers*. Thames & Hudson, London and Wiley, Hoboken, 2005

Borden, Gail Peter and Michael Meredith, et al. *Matter: Material Processes in Architectural Production*. Routledge, London, 2011

Borden, Gail Peter. *Material Precedent: the Typology of Modern Tectonics*. Wiley, Hoboken, 2010

Brownell, Blaine. *Material Strategies: Innovative Applications in Architecture (Architecture Brief)*. Princeton Architectural Press, New York, 2011

Deplazes, Andrea and and Gerd H. Söffker. *Constructing Architecture: Materials, Processes, Structures, a Handbook*. Wiley, Hoboken, 2010

Iwamoto, Lisa. *Digital Fabrications: Architectural and Material Techniques (Architecture Briefs)*. Princeton Architectural Press, New York, 2009

Kolarevic, Branko and Kevin Klinger. *Manufacturing Material Effects: Rethinking Design and Making in Architecture*. Routledge, London and New York, 2008

McMorrough, Julia. *Materials, Structures, and Standards: All the Details Architects Need to Know But Can Never Find*. Rockport, Gloucester, Mass., 2006

Meisel, Ari. *LEED Materials: A Resource Guide to Green Building*. Princeton Architectural Press, New York, 2010

Mori, Toshiko. *Immaterial/Ultramaterial: Architecture, Design, and Materials (Millennium Matters)*. George Braziller, New York, 2002

Murray, Scott. *Translucent Building Skins: Material Innovations in Modern and Contemporary Architecture*. Routledge, London, 2012

Onouye, Barry S. and Kevin Kane. *Statics and Strength of Materials for Architecture and Building Construction* (4th edition). Prentice Hall, Harlow, 2011

Oxman, Rivka and Robert Oxman, et al. *The New Structuralism: Design, Engineering and Architectural Technologies (Architectural Design)*. Wiley, Hoboken, 2010

Peters, Sascha. *Material Revolution. Sustainable and Multi-Purpose Materials for Design and Architecture*. Birkhäuser, Basel, 2011

The Phaidon Atlas of 21st Century World Architecture. Phaidon Press, London, 2008

Ritter, Axel. *Smart Materials in Architecture, Interior Architecture and Design*. Birkhäuser, Basel and Boston, 2006

Salvadori, Mario. *The Art of Construction: Projects and Principles for Beginning Engineers and Architects*. Chicago Review Press, Chicago, 2000

Sauer, Christiane. *Made of: New Materials Sourcebook for Architecture and Design*. Gestalten Verlag, Berlin, 2010

Stang, Alanna and Christopher Hawthorne. *The Green House: New Directions in Sustainable Architecture*. Princeton Architectural Press, New York, 2010

Ternaux, Elodie. *Material World 3: Innovative Materials for Architecture and Design*. Frame Publishers, Amsterdam, 2011

20th-Century World Architecture. Phaidon Press, London, 2012

Van Uffelen, Chris. *Pure Plastics: New Materials for Today's Architecture*. Verlagshaus Braun, Berlin, 2008

Wigginton, Michael. *Glass in Architecture*. Phaidon, London, 2002

GLOSSARY

aerogel
A glass foam that is among the lightest and most thermally insulating solids ever produced. Also known as "solid smoke" or "frozen smoke," it is produced by the "sol-gel" method (a process of producing solid materials from very small molecules).

ALC (autoclaved lightweight concrete)
A porous, highly thermally insulating concrete-based material used for building construction. Panels and bricks are manufactured using very fine aggregate (sand or fly ash waste generated from thermal power plants). A key advantage is easy installation since the material can be routed, sanded, or cut to size on site using standard carbon-steel power tools.

aramid
A hybrid of nylon, aramids are high-performance yarns and fabrics that offer exceptional fire retardance and impact absorption, as with fire suits and bullet-proof vests.

cermet
Ceramic particles held together by a metal binder. The composite uses the ductile nature of metals (aluminum, nickel, or molybdenum) to bond hard, stiff particles and fibers of SiC (silicon carbide) or TiN (titanium nitride). This synergistic combination is ideal for such uses as tough, hard drill bits, cutting tools, and bioceramic hip replacements.

cerused oak
A finish where the porous open grain of oak planks is washed with a white paste revealing the grain lines but leaving the overall color of the wood unchanged. Similar to limed oak, which involves rubbing finely crushed limestone over raw oak so that the open-grained pores pick up the limestone particles, highlighting the wood.

CNC milling
CNC—Computer Numerical Control—refers to any milling process that is directed by a digital program, rather than manually.

elastic modulus
Refers to a material's resistance to deforming elastically when force is applied to it, and then returning to its original shape after the force is removed. The force can be tensile (pulling), shear (top and bottom surfaces pulled in opposing directions), bending, or torsional (twisting).

ETFE (ethylene tetrafluoroethylene)
A lightweight, transparent fluoropolymer plastic film that resists outdoor conditions (UV light, acid rain, seawater, bacteria) as well as tearing and impact.

FRP (fiber-reinforced plastic)
A family of thermoplastics (nylon, polypropylene, and PVC) as well as thermosets (epoxy and polyester) that are reinforced with stiffening fibers and fabric. These include glass, carbon fiber, and natural materials, such as flax and hemp. The fibers are added during the molding process when the polymer is semi-liquid.

FSC (Forest Stewardship Council)
An international non-profit organization promoting responsible, sustainable management of the world's forests via use of a global certification system for forests and forest products.

furan
A colorless, volatile liquid compound that is obtained from the wood oils of pines, or made synthetically and used for organic synthesis.

glulam (glued laminated timber)
A structural timber product composed of individual wood laminations, or "lams," specifically selected and positioned in the timber for their performance characteristics and then bonded together with durable, moisture-resistant adhesives.

GRP (glass-reinforced plastic/glass-fibre-reinforced plastic)
A composite material made of plastic reinforced with fine glass fibers. These can be short (0.5–1 mm), long (3–6 mm), woven mats, or pultruded fibers (pulled and extruded). Typically thermoset plastics, such as epoxy resins, are used and laid up by hand, placing the fiber mats or fabrics in position before rolling on epoxy resins to stiffen the part.

LEED (Leadership in Energy and Environmental Design)
A ratings system developed by the US Green Building Council for the encouragement and certification of environmentally responsible design and construction worldwide.

PET, PETE (polyethylene terephthalate)
The chemical name for polyester used in most fabric fibers and in beverage bottles as well as on some food packaging.

PLA (polylactic acid)
A polyester-like plastic produced from the polymerization of renewable resources such as cornstarch, tapioca, and sugar cane. It is certified as industrially compostable, and is used in packaging and as a fiber for fabrics.

polyolefin
The family of thermoplastics, often referred to as commodity thermoplastics, that includes the widely used polypropylene and polyethylene. Polyolefins means "oil-like," in reference to the oily or waxy feel of these materials.

PTFE (polytetrafluoroethylene)
A fluoropolymer (contains fluorine) that is best known by its brand name: Teflon. It is durable; resistant to UV, acids, and bases; and both oleophobic (oil aversion) and hydrophobic (water aversion). The result is a very soil-resistant and non-stick plastic, which is commonly used as a non-stick coating for pans and other cookware.

PVB (polyvinyl butyral)
A transparent printable safety film, used chiefly as the interlayer between laminated glass. Polyvinyl butyral is in the same family of plastics as PVC, but does not contain chlorine. It is UV-stable, optically clear, and tear-resistant.

seat cut
The horizontal notch cut into the underside of a rafter beam for joining the roof of a building to its vertical outer wall.

shagreen
The rough skin of certain sharks and rays that is often used as a decorative material. Also, a rough grainy leather made from the rump of certain animal hides.

silica fume
Also known as microsilica, an ultrafine glass powder that is a by-product of producing silicon metal and ferrosilicon alloys for industrial use. It is often used as an aggregate in concrete for its ability to enhance the material's bond and compressive strength.

spandrel
The almost triangular space between the curve of an arch and its rectangular enclosure. In a building with more than one floor, spandrel refers to the space between the top of the window in one story and the sill of the window in the story above it.

standing seam
The raised ridge where two metal sheets meet on a paneled roof, enhancing overall weather resistance.

SIP (structural insulated panel)
A high-performance building panel that consists of an insulating foam core sandwiched between two structural boards. Strong and energy-efficient, SIPs fulfill several aspects of conventional building, such as studs and joists, insulation, and vapor and air barriers, and function as exterior wall, roof, floor, and foundation systems.

UHPC (ultra-high-performance concrete)
A new class of high-strength, high-durability concretes whose compositions and casting regimens have been tightly controlled to maximize performance. Constituent materials include Portland cement, silica fume, quartz flour, fine silica sand, high-range water-reducer, water, and either steel or organic fibers.

Voronoi diagram
A method of dividing or partitioning a two- or three-dimensional space into a number of polygon regions such that each one contains a single generating point and every point in a region is closer to its companion generating points than to any other. The regions or cells are called Voronoi polygons.

CONTRIBUTOR CONTACTS

ALA Architects
Tehtaankatu 40 B 17
00150 Helsinki
Finland
T: 358 9 4259 7330
E: info@ala.fi
www.ala.fi

Alliance Arkitekter AS
Kristian Augusts Gate 13
0164 Oslo
Norway
T: 47 22 36 40 44

Kvitsøygata 23
4014 Stravanger
Norway
T: 47 45 03 62 18
E: en@allark.no
www.allark.net

Arcagency
Mads Møller (founder of MAPT)
Gasværksvej 8d, 1
1656 Copenhagen
Denmark
T: 45 61 28 00 12
E: moller@arcagency.com
www.arcagency.com

Arquitectos Anónimos
Rua Anselmo Braancamp
No. 29–2 Esq. Tras.
4000-083 Porto
Portugal
T: 351 2 2502 4161
E: info@arquitectosanonimos.com
www.arquitectosanonimos.com

Atelier Tekuto
4-1-20-B1F Jingumae
Shibuya-ku
Tokyo 150-0001
Japan
T: 81 3 6439 5540
E: info@tekuto.com
www.tekuto.com

Benthem Crouwel Architects
Benthem Crouwel Architekten BV bna
Generaal Vetterstraat 61
1059 BT Amsterdam
The Netherlands
T: 31 20 642 01 05
E: info@benthemcrouwel.nl

Benthem Crouwel GmbH
Bendstraße 50–52
52066 Aachen
Germany
T: 49 241 559 45 0
www.benthemcrouwel.nl

Billings Design Associates
Unit 9, The Hyde Building
The Park, Carrickmines, Dublin 18
Ireland
T: 35 3 1 294 0060
E: info@billingsdesign.ie
www.billingsdesign.ie

BogermanDill
Donker Curtiusstraat 7
1051 JL Amsterdam
The Netherlands
T: 31 20 684 77 77
E: info@bogermandill.nl
www.bogermandill.nl

Gail Peter Borden, RA, AIA, NCARB
Borden Partnership LLP
Los Angeles, CA 90089
United States
T: 1 919 455 1053
E: gborden@usc.edu
www.bordenpartnership.com

David Chipperfield Architects
11 York Road
London SE1 7NX
United Kingdom
T: 44 20 7620 4800
E: info@davidchipperfield.co.uk

Gesellschaft von Architekten mbH
Joachimstrasse 11
10119 Berlin
Germany
T: 49 30 280 170 0
E: info@davidchipperfield.de
www.davidchipperfield.co.uk

Designed by Erick van Egeraat
Calandstraat 23
3016 CA Rotterdam
The Netherlands
T: 31 10 436 96 86
E: info@erickvanegeraat.com
www.erickvanegeraat.com

designtoproduction
Seestrasse 78
8703 Erlenbach/Zurich
Switzerland
T: 41 44 914 74 90
E: info@designtoproduction.com
www.designtoproduction.ch

Dietrich Schwarz Architekten AG
ETH/SIA
Seefeldstrasse 224
8008 Zurich
Switzerland
T: 41 44 389 10 60
E: info@schwarz-architekten.com
www.schwarz-architektur.ch

DOSU Studio Architecture
Doris Kim Sung
8 Buggy Whip Drive
Rolling Hills, CA 90274
United States
T: 1 310 722 4458
E: doris@dosu-arch.com
www.dosu-arch.com

Foster + Partners
Riverside
22 Hester Road
London SW11 4AN
United Kingdom
T: 44 20 7738 0455
E: info@fosterandpartners.com
www.fosterandpartners.com

FR-EE Fernando Romero Enterprise
511 25th St. 901
New York, NY 10010
United States
T: 1 212 242 3104
E: hv@fr-ee.org

Plaza Carso, Piso 14
Lago Zurich No. 245,
Edificio Presa Falcón
Col. Ampliación Granada
Miguel Hidalgo
11520, D.F
Mexico
T: 52 55 26141060 ext. 121
www.fr-ee.org

Gehry Technologies
12541-A Beatrice Street
Los Angeles, CA 90066
United States
T: 1 310 862 1200

150 West 30th Street, 4th Floor
New York, NY 10001
United States
T: 1 212 239 9288
www.gehrytechnologies.com

Hariri Pontarini Architects
602 King Street West
Toronto, M5V 1M6
Canada
T: 1 416 929 4901
E: info@hp-arch.com
www.hariripontarini.com

Heatherwick Studio
356–64 Gray's Inn Road
London WC1X 8BH
United Kingdom
T: 44 20 7833 8800
E: studio@heatherwick.com
www.heatherwick.com

Herzog & de Meuron
Rheinschanze 6
4056 Basel
Switzerland
T: 41 61 385 5757
E: info@herzogdemeuron.com
www.herzogdemeuron.com

Hugh Broughton Architects
41A Beavor Lane
London W6 9BL
United Kingdom
T: 44 20 8735 9959
E: info@hbarchitects.co.uk
www.hbarchitects.co.uk

Jakob + Macfarlane Architects
13–15 rue des Petites Ecuries
75010 Paris
France
T: 33 1 44 79 05 72
E: info@jacobmacfarlane.com
www.jakmak1.dotster.com

Jean de Gastines Architectes
87 rue de la Verrerie
75004 Paris
France
T: 33 1 42 78 23 21
E: agence@degastines.com
www.jdg-architectes.com

Asif Kahn
1–5 Vyner Street
London E2 9DG
United Kingdom
T: 44 20 8980 3685
E: studio@asif-khan.com
www.asif-khan.com

Kengo Kuma & Associates
2-24-8 BY-CUBE 2F
Miniamiaoyama
Minato-ku Tokyo 107-0062
Japan
T: 81 3 3401 7721
E: kuma@kkaa.co.jp

16 rue Martel
75010 Paris
France
T: 33 1 44 88 94 90
www.kkaa.co.jp

KieranTimberlake
420 North 20th Street
Philadelphia, PA 19130-3828
United States
T: 1 215 922 6600
E: timberlake@kierantimberlake.com
www.kierantimberlake.com

LAVA
72 Campbell Street
Sydney NSW 2010
Australia
T: 61 292801475
E: directors@l-a-v-a.net
www.l-a-v-a.net

Lendager Arkitekter
Anders Lendager (founder of MAPT)
Grøntorvet 280 1 Th.
2500 Valby
Denmark
T: 45 61 28 00 90
E: info@lendagerark.dk
www.lendagerark.dk

MAD Architects
3rd Floor West Tower
No. 7 Banqiao Nanxiang, Beixinqiao
Beijing 100007
China
T: 86 10 64026632
E: office@i-mad.com
www.i-mad.com

Magma Architecture
Charlottenstrasse 95
10969 Berlin
Germany
T: 49 30 259 229 70
E: info@magmaarchitecture.com
www.magmaarchitecture.com

Manuelle Gautrand Architecture
36 boulevard de la Bastille
75012 Paris
France
T: 33 1 56 95 06 46
E: contact@manuelle-gautrand.com
www.manuelle-gautrand.com

Morphosis Architects
3440 Wesley Street
Culver City, CA 90232
United States
T: 1 424 258 6200

153 West 27th Street #1200
New York, NY 10001
United States
T: 1 212 675 1100
E: studio@morphosis.net
www.morphosis.com

Neutelings Riedijk Architects
P.O. Box 527
3000 AM Rotterdam
The Netherlands
T: 31 10 404 66 77
E: info@neutelings-riedijk.com
www.neutelings-riedijk.com

NEX Architecture
Alan Dempsey
71 Newman Street
London W1T 3EQ
United Kingdom
T: 44 20 7183 0900
E: office@nex-architecture.com
www.nex-architecture.com

Pernilla Ohrstedt
E: studio@pernilla-ohrstedt.com

Pohl Architekten
Bergstromweg 4
99094 Erfurt
Germany
T: 49 03 614 302 52 60
E: info@pohlarchitekten.de
www.pohlarchitekten.de

REX
20 Jay Street Suite 920
Brooklyn, NY 11201
United States
T: 1 646 230 6557
E: office@rex-ny.com
www.rex-ny.com

Gernot Riether
School of Architecture
Georgia Institute of Technology
247 4th St. Suite 351
Atlanta, Georgia 30332
United States
T: 1 404 889 3274
E: gernot.riether@coa.gatech.edu

Enric Ruiz-Geli & Cloud 9
Passatge Mercador 10 bajos 32
08008 Barcelona
Spain
T: 34 93 215 05 53
E: info@e-cloud9.com
www.e-cloud9.com
www.ruiz-geli.com

Sandow
3651 NW 8th Ave
Boca Raton, FL 33431
United States
T: 1 561 961 7600
www.sandow.com

SDA | Synthesis Design + Architecture
Alvin Huang
2404 Wilshire Boulevard Suite 9E
Los Angeles, CA 90057
United States
T: 1 213 438 9967

Unit 2.6 Rockwell House,
10–14 Hewett Street
London EC2A 3NN
United Kingdom
T: 44 20 7193 7263
E: studio@synthesis-dna.com
www.synthesis-dna.com

Kazuyo Sejima & Ryue Nishizawa / SANAA
1-5-27, Tatsumi
Koto-ku, Tokyo 135-0053
Japan
T: 81 3 5534 1780
E: sanaa@sanaa.co.jp
www.sanaa.co.jp

Shigeru Ban Architects
5-2-4 Matsubara, Setagaya
Tokyo 156-0043
Japan
T: 81 3 3324 6760
E: tokyo@shigerubanarchitects.com

Shigeru Ban Architects Europe
6 rue de Braque
75003 Paris
France
T: 33 1 70 71 20 50
E: europe@shigerubanarchitects.com
www.shigerubanarchitects.com

Steven Holl Architects
450 West 31st Street, 11th floor
New York, NY 10001
United States
T: 1 212 629 7262
E: nyc@stevenholl.com

1 Xiangheyuan Road, Wanguocheng
Building 1-106, Dongcheng District
Beijing 100028
China
T: 86 10 84408551
E: beijing@stevenholl.com
www.stevenholl.com

Superuse Studios
Emantspad 5
3061 CE Rotterdam
The Netherlands
T: 31 10 466 44 44
E: info@superuse-studios.com
www.superuse-studios.com

THEVERYMANY
E: fornesmarc@gmail.com
www.theverymany.com

UNStudio
Stadhouderskade 113
1073 AX Amsterdam
The Netherlands
T: 31 20 570 20 40
E: info@unstudio.com

Room 4606
Raffles City, No. 268
Xizang Middle Road
Shanghai 200001
China
T: 86 21 63405088
E: asia@unstudio.com
www.unstudio.com

Waugh Thistleton Architects
74 Paul Street
London EC2A 4NA
United Kingdom
T: 44 20 7613 5727
E: info@waughthistleton.com
www.waughthistleton.com

Zaha Hadid Architects
10 Bowling Green Lane
London EC1R 0BQ
United Kingdom
T: 44 20 7253 5247
E: press@zaha-hadid.com
www.zaha-hadid.com

Zieta Prozessdesign
Ferdinand-Hodler-Strasse 16
8049 Zurich, Switzerland

Ul. Moniuszki 29/2
51-610 Wroclaw
Poland
E: info@zieta.pl
www.zieta.pl

Material ConneXion®
1271 Avenue of the Americas
17th Floor
New York, NY 10020
United States
T: 1 212 842 2050
E: info@materialconnexion.com
www.materialconnexion.com

Material ConneXion® Bangkok
Bangkok, Thailand
www.materialconnexion.com/th

Material ConneXion® Beijing
Beijing, China
www.materialconnexion.cn

Material ConneXion® Cologne
Cologne, Germany
www.materialconnexion.com/de

Material ConneXion® Daegu
Daegu, Republic of Korea
www.materialconnexion.com/kr

Material ConneXion® Istanbul
Istanbul, Turkey
www.materialconnexion.com/tr

Material ConneXion® Italia
Milan, Italy
www.materialconnexion.com/it

Material ConneXion® Rio de Janiero
Rio de Janiero, Brazil
www.materialconnexion.com/br

Material ConneXion® Seoul
Seoul, Republic of Korea
www.seoul.materialconnexion.com

Material ConneXion® Shanghai
Shanghai, China
www.materialconnexion.cn

Material ConneXion® Skövde
Skövde, Sweden
www.materialconnexion.com/se

Material ConneXion® Tokyo
Tokyo, Japan
www.materialconnexion.com/jp

While this series is intended for both the academic and the professional reader, its primary goal is to reveal for the young practitioner the extraordinary range of advanced materials and their influence on the creative process. This knowledge provides the foundation for how to use materials as a vehicle for addressing many of today's creative challenges.

Each chapter is separated by a spread in the form of a visual narrative. The purpose of these pages is to graphically depict the journey a designer takes from conception to completed design, recognizing that engagement with a material is part of an extended process of exploration and invention. These pages have been generously provided by a handful of outstanding individuals and firms that, in many cases, have produced a body of work that reflects their intimate working knowledge of a particular material type or process. Our hope is that by acknowledging the exploratory process inspired by the possibilities of material science, especially as they apply to a specific commission or set of conditions, we can foster greater material innovation across all creative disciplines.

HARIRI PONTARINI ARCHITECTS (PAGE 8)

Toronto, Santiago

This timeline-tableau illustrates "controlled abandon": the exploration of the design for the Bahá'í Temple of South America through hand sketching, model-making, digital design techniques, and digital technologies. This collaborative task drew on numerous sources and was informed by physical form-finding experiments. It allowed for a synthesis of new developments, with one medium informing another, and the concept of light—physically and spiritually—as a constant design inspiration. It led the architects to delve into the possibilities of creating a building that would capture the relationship between space and light, movement and stillness.

STEVEN HOLL ARCHITECTS (PAGE 18)

New York, Beijing, San Francisco

Throughout history, the golden ratio (or 1:1.618 ratio for length to width of rectangles) has been considered the most pleasing to the eye. Architects and artists have continually used this proportion, and it is present in the work of 2012 AIA Gold Medalist Steven Holl. The architect uses the golden ratio to determine proportions and details, the scale of openings and spatial sequences, even furnishings. This approach ensures that every aspect of a building is carefully considered in relation to the whole and corresponds to the search for a deeper experience of time, space, light, and materials.

KENGO KUMA & ASSOCIATES (PAGE 56)

Tokyo, Paris

Identifying the appropriate size of a particle (unit) for the site is essential in the architects' design. They carefully study how big or small the element is that comprises the entire site (like the accumulation of cells that make a human body), and how it could match and merge with its environment. The very process of deciding on the particle takes up a large part of their work.

ZAHA HADID ARCHITECTS (PAGE 94)

London, Hamburg

The design of Heydar Aliyev Centre establishes a continuous, fluid relationship between the external plaza and the center's interior, where the public are drawn into the building in a seamless gesture, thus blurring the line between architecture and urban landscape, figure and ground, interior and exterior, private and public. The materiality allows them to generate a series of undulations, bifurcations, folds, and inflections, which modify the artificial landscape of the plaza to create a surface that performs a multitude of functions—welcoming, embracing, and directing all visitors throughout the various levels of the interior.

MORPHOSIS ARCHITECTS (PAGE 128)

Culver City, New York

The performance-driven designs by Morphosis connect architecture, engineering, fabrication, and construction. Both sculptural and functional, the building skins respond to the orientation of the sun, minimize heat gain, and maximize interior exposures to natural daylight. The play of opacity and transparency improves overall energy efficiency and user comfort while maintaining views of the city.

LAVA (PAGE 166)

Sydney, Stuttgart, Berlin, Shanghai

LAVA (Laboratory for Visionary Architecture) put a premium on biomimicry, as is evident in their louver-like system of images that span the creative process. Their preference for intelligent systems and skins seeks to align architecture with the responsiveness of the natural world. By exploring the complex three-dimensional geometry of forms in nature, they aim to incorporate buildability into the form from inception through parametric modeling techniques. LAVA is man, nature, and technology.

UNSTUDIO (PAGE 196)

Amsterdam, Hong Kong, Shanghai

This selection of images from two media façade designs for luxury shopping plazas in South Korea—the Galleria Department Store in Seoul and the Galleria Centercity in Cheonan—outlines the various stages of the design-build process, from inspirations, concepts, sketching, model-making, material testing and mock-up production to the final solutions and materials applied in the buildings. The high degree of experimentation and testing involved in the production of both projects highlights the research and prototyping that are necessary to find the optimal solutions required to turn design concepts into physical reality.

PICTURE CREDITS

a = above
b = below
c = center
l = left
r = right

1: credits for images on this page are listed under the relevant projects; 2–3: © Hufton + Crow / VIEW; 6: credits for images on this page are listed under the relevant projects; 8–9: Hariri Pontarini Architects; 10, 13, 14, 17: Luke Gibson Photography; 18–19: © Iwan Baan, Andy Ryan, Steven Holl Architects; 20: Hariri Pontarini Architects; 22: used with permission from Microsoft.; 23: Image Courtesy of Corning Inc.; 25, 27a: © Iwan Baan; 26al: © SANAA; 27b: Damian Wohrer/ Kinopicz American; 29b: Christian Richters; 29a, 30–31: © Ute Zscharnt for David Chipperfield Architects; 33a, 33b, 34a, 34b, 35b: © Iwan Baan; 35a: REX; 37, 38a, 38b, 39a, 39b: © Richard Bryant / Arcaid.co.uk; 41, 42a, 42cr, 42-43: Gaston Wicky; 42cl, 42b: GlassX AG, Zurich; 45, 46b, 47a, 47b: Sas Glas – Saint Gobain, photo: Marc Detiff; 46a: © Iwan Baan; 49, 50, 51a, 51b: © Peter Aaron / OTTO; 53al, 53bl, 53br: Hariri Pontarini Architects; 53ar: Gartner Steel and Glass GmbH; 54–55: rendering by Hariri Pontarini Architects with Mark Cichy; 56–57: Kengo Kuma & Associates; 58: Courtesy of Perennial Wood; 61a, 61b: MIO; 62, 64al, 64cl: D2P (designtoproduction GmbH); 63, 65a, 65b: Tuomas Uusheimo; 64bl: Trebyggeriet; 67al (all four images), 67b: © Superuse Studios; 67ar, 68–69: Allard van der Hoek; 71a, 71b, 72, 73: Ivo Canelas; 75a, 76b: © Wil van Iersel; 75b, 76a, 77: Courtesy BogermanDill Architecten; 79, 80, 81al, 81ar, 81b: Toshihiro Sobajima; 83, 84a, 84b, 85a, 85b: © Terje Skåre; 87, 89: Will Pryce / Arcaid.co.uk; 88a, 88b: © KLH; 91, 92b, 93: Santi Caleca; 92al: drawing by Shigeru Ban Architects; 94–95: Zaha Hadid Architects; 96: 3D Systems, Bespoke Products; 98: Courtesy of Material ConneXion; 99: Siemens press picture; 101al, 101ac, 101ar, 102: Pohl Architekten; 101b, 103: © Roland Halbe; 105a, 105bl, 105br: photo: Dave Vickers; 106–107: UNStudio; 109, 111: © Christian Richters; 110: © J. Collingridge; 113a, 113b, 114a, 115a, 115b: Andy Cheatle; 114b: diagram by Hugh Broughton Architects; 117, 118b, 119: NEX Architecture; 118al: drawing by NEX Architecture; 118ar: diagram by NEX Architecture; 121, 122br, 123a, 123b: © Max Lerouge – LMCU; 122a, 122bl: Manuelle Gautrand Architecture; 125a, 125b, 126–27: © Jannes Linders; 128–29: Morphosis Architects; 130: Simyo Gallery / Jang Yong Sun; 132a: Arcam AB; 132b: Joris Laarman Lab; 133: Courtesy of iGuzzini, photo: Adrià Goula; 135, 136b, 137: © Jakob + Macfarlane Architects, photo: Nicolas Borel; 136a: diagram by Jakob + Macfarlane Architects; 139, 140al, 140ar, 140bl, 140br, 141: © Roland Halbe; 143a, 143b: MAD Architects; 144–45: © Iwan Baan; 147a, 147b, 148–49: © Brandon Shigeta; 151, 152al, 152b: Gehry Technologies; 152ar, 153a: Adam Weisman; 153b: Rafael Gamo; 155a, 155b, 156–157: SUSHISAMBA; 158, 160al, 160ar, 160b, 161: Zieta Prozessdesign; 159: photo: geeLy; 163al, 163ar, 163b, 164–65: © Andy Stagg / VIEW; 166–67: LAVA; 168: flickr © carlbob "Olympic Stadium Wrap - detail"; 170al, 170ar: North Technology Group LLC; 171: Courtesy Microsoft/MIT; 173, 174a, 174b, 175: © Dirk Wilhelmy / Artur / VIEW; 176–77: © Hufton + Crow; 178a: © Hufton + Crow / VIEW; 178b: Magma Architecture; 179: © J.L. Diehl; 181a: Enric Ruiz Geli © Cloud 9; 181b, 183bl, 183br: Luis Ros © Cloud 9; 182: © Gunnar Knechtel; 183a: José Miguel Hernandez © Cloud 9; 185, 186a, 187a: © Hufton + Crow / VIEW; 186b: Gareth Cattermole / Getty Images Entertainment; 187b: © Hufton + Crow; 189, 190, 191: © Nigel Young / Foster + Partners; 193, 195al, 195ar, 195bl, 195br: © Gernot Riether; 194: diagram by Gernot Riether; 196–97: UNStudio; 200–215: all images in the Materials Directory courtesy of Material ConneXion

224

THE AUTHORS

Dr. Andrew H. Dent, Vice President, Library & Materials Research, plays a key role in the expansion of Material ConneXion's technical knowledge base. His research directs the implementation of consulting projects and the selection of innovative, sustainable, and advanced materials for Material ConneXion's Library, which to date contains more than 7,000 materials. From Whirlpool and Adidas to BMW and Proctor & Gamble, Dr. Dent has helped numerous Fortune 500 companies develop or improve their products through the use of innovative materials. A prominent speaker, he has presented at many international events on sustainable and innovative material strategies. He has contributed to numerous publications and is co-author of *Ultra Materials: How Materials Innovation is Changing the World* and *Material ConneXion: The Global Resource of New and Innovative Materials for Architects, Artists and Designers*. He received his Ph.D. in Materials Science from Cambridge University in Britain.

Leslie Sherr is a New York-based editor and author who focuses on architecture, design, and gardens. For more than two decades she has written on new directions in multiple fields of design and worked as a brand strategist for such leading communication design firms as C&G Partners, Carbone Smolan Agency, Assouline, and Desgrippes Gobé & Associates. She studied critical writing on architecture and design, and has a Bachelor of Fine Arts from SUNY Purchase as well as a Master of Science in Landscape Design from Columbia University. A Francophile, she believes that beauty is the world's great civilizing force and that artfully crafted books can open our eyes and expand our minds.

Material ConneXion (materialconnexion.com) is a global materials and innovation consultancy that helps clients create the products and services of tomorrow through smart materials and design thinking. Material ConneXion, a Sandow company, is the trusted adviser to Fortune 500 companies, as well as to any forward-thinking agencies and government entities seeking a creative, competitive, or sustainable edge. With eleven locations—in Bangkok, Beijing, Cologne, Daegu, Istanbul, Milan, New York, Seoul, Shanghai, Skövde, and Tokyo—Material ConneXion's international network of specialists provides a global, cross-industry perspective on materials, design, new product development, sustainability and innovation. Material ConneXion maintains the world's largest subscription-based materials library, with more than 7,000 innovative materials and processes—an indispensable asset to a wide audience of users. The consulting division, ThinkLab, works with clients to strategically incorporate trends, service and innovation into their business models and products, while sister company Culture + Commerce represents the world's leading designers, including Philippe Starck and Marcel Wanders, in licensing their groundbreaking new products and projects.

ACKNOWLEDGMENTS

Although we appear as the authors of this book, it is in fact the work of many hands. The project has been in every sense a team effort, which would not have been possible without the vision of George M. Beylerian, founder of Material ConneXion, together with the knowledge, skills, hard work, and dedication of many colleagues.

The book is the culmination of many people's work and we would like to take this opportunity to thank those who were most closely connected with the project. We are grateful to Michele Caniato, president, for bringing Material ConneXion and Thames & Hudson together to realize the full potential of this ambitious project, and to Adam I. Sandow, founder, chairman, and chief executive officer of Sandow, for his support. Our extended thanks go to the Material ConneXion marketing department – Gabriella Vivaldi, William Nichols, Carlo Grioli and Daniel Swartz, Assistant Editor – for working tirelessly to help bring this book to life. For his guidance: Matthew Kalishman; for contributing to the editorial team: Tiffany Vasilchik, Maider Irastorza, Fiona Anastas, Elizabeth Peterson, Sarah Hoit, and Alejandra Kluger. Thank you also to the sales team at Material ConneXion who have given their time and resources and whose dedication is reflected in these pages.

We owe a special debt to all the outstanding architects and architectural firms whose visions have so enriched our understanding of what is materially possible in the ever-thrilling field of architecture, and who have given so generously of their time, knowledge, and insight, especially Gail Peter Borden for his introduction to this volume. Our endless thanks also go out to the many contributors, including photographers, media contacts, scientists, and manufacturers, whose creativity, research, and knowledge underpin every chapter in the book. It has not been possible here, for reasons of space, to include every single individual by name, but that does not lessen our gratitude to them.

Material Innovation has been created in collaboration with Thames & Hudson. Without Jamie Camplin's championing, this series would not have happened. We would like to extend our warmest appreciation to him, as well as to Ilona de Nemethy Sanigar, who offered invaluable direction and is a genuine pleasure to work with. We are also grateful to Johanna Neurath, design director, and Samuel Clark, senior designer, for the publication design, to Kirsty Seymour-Ure for her sensitive copyediting, and to Paul Hammond for his production control.

Andrew H. Dent
Leslie Sherr